Religion of Buddhism for the 21st Century

Patrick Boardman

Published by Patrick Boardman, 2021.

While every precaution has been taken in the preparation of this book, the publisher assumes no responsibility for errors or omissions, or for damages resulting from the use of the information contained herein.

RELIGION OF BUDDHISM FOR THE 21ST CENTURY

First edition. February 17, 2021.

Copyright © 2021 Patrick Boardman.

ISBN: 979-8223880905

Written by Patrick Boardman.

Introduction

Siddhartha Gautama the Buddha lived in a society where people were mostly atheists or traditional polytheists accustomed to stories of many gods. There is no mention of God's existence or non-existence in Buddha's teachings because no one at that time would have listened. There are no Scriptural quotes from God in Buddhism. Topics like the Underworld and Enlightenment are spiritual matters of great importance to mankind, so it is time to redefine the Religion of Buddhism as a monotheistic religion without any doubt of God's existence in light of scripture coming to civilization since the days of Buddha, and new knowlege of Quantum Theory. There are four ages mentioned in Buddhist, Taoist, Muslim, and Biblical writings, and this is the Final Age of mankind .

Philosophers and Zen scholars have displayed a humanistic zeal to avoid acknowledging the Supreme Being as the Creator of all things. No one should worship Buddha as God since God does not take human form. The Creator is omnipresent, infinite, and invisible. This book will outline the truth of existence, the correct spiritual doctrine of monotheism. Consciousness is everything, so it is logical to assume we are alive for a reason. The path to Enlightenment must have a destination. The place we yearn for is eternal Paradise, the state of reward that will be given only to those souls who are pure enough to deserve it.

People are seldom open minded; the human ego insists on being right about all things. Fixed beliefs and confrontational attitudes are dangerous to the soul since new information will go unheeded. Mankind is hostile to any ideas that go against their rigid mentality. The goal of life should be enlightenment. Faith is admirable, but blind faith in false doctrines leads to destruction. Flexibility of thought and purity of intention are virtues that will lead to the great reward in the Afterlife in Heaven. A person must have the open-minded innocence of a child to achieve eternal happiness. A wise person learns modesty, respect, and self-discipline. Awareness can be heightened and expanded through techniques such as Yoga, Martial Arts, fasting, meditation, and when under the influence of organic hallucinogens such as peyote or magic mushrooms. It is wise to heed all available knowledge that has come to us since the days of Buddha, who lived four centuries before Christ. There are evil forces in the world that affect us negatively, so we must decide how to resist those who want to rule the world and who seek to enslave populations and poison our bodies so that people will become progressively weaker and die faster..

It is important for all philosophical, political, and religious entities to understand that there has always been a high degree of accuracy in the prophetic verses of Judeo-Christian and Islamic Scripture. The rivalry amongst major religions has caused war, hatred, and oppression of others. The animosity between cultures is contrary to the values that should be practiced by spiritual people. There is also widespread scorn for the very idea of a Supreme Being: atheism is common although science has proven that there is an omnipresent and conscious Creator of all things. To make matters worse, the Vatican has opened several temples of "Chrislam" designed to absorb all major religions into one world religion under the leadership of the pope of Rome. If the New World Order succeeds, the monolithic one world government will have a unified set of laws, and all citizens will be forced to convert to the only legal religion in order to buy and sell goods. The globalists motivate people into compliance by creating mass movements through fear campaigns, and religions can be used to control populations.

Declaring oneself a Buddhist is not likely to cancel out evil surroundings, for we are affected by the physical environment and those who are alive around us who cause misery to others. Those who have increased awareness through disciplined concentration will find that their thoughts and intentions help to shape events along the trail favorably. A person encounters danger at times, which requires action to survive threats or to make right something that is wrong. The Day of Judgment will be common to all human beings. The Creator has promised this in His communications with mankind over the centuries. There are recent messages that will change everything for the better if mankind heeds the warning. The fools who control the physical world are determined to provoke another world war; this could lead to complete destruction.

I will explain how I obtained the knowledge presented in this book, and why I wield the authority to make such statements. I first learned about Buddhism around the year 1962, when I dropped out of the Catholic church. The education in the separate schools was very good, but I could not take part in the idol worship nor the complex rituals, such as reenacting the crucifixion endlessly, so that participants are drawn into feelings of sympathy and guilt – the emotions which priests use to entice donations from the flock.

Buddhists follow the Dalai Lama as their leader, but he teaches that it does not matter whether a person believes in God or not, so he is not a religious leader. He is a politician appointed into his position who is trying to please as many people as possible by allowing atheism to be an acceptable doctrine. To have any meaning, all religions must have a God, definitions of sin, and the belief in an eternal reward or punishment. People commit crimes because they believe they will get away without punishment after death, which is wishful thinking.

Many people just want to worship nature, without acknowledging there is a Creator to all existence. That line of thought is materialistic, not spiritual. We live in a temporary situation that will be changed drastically before long. All people will be transformed into pure consciousness on the Last Day. Those souls who have failed to understand the meaning of life will miss out on the reward.

The Four Noble Truths

The Sanskrit word 'dukkha' encompasses suffering, painful experiences, and things that cannot be satisfied. The First Noble Truth is that these are innate characteristics of Samsara, the worldly life and rebirth cycle.

The Second Noble Truth is 'samudaya', which refers to the cause of suffering. The concept is called 'tanha', which means 'craving'. This includes attachment to pleasures of the senses, trying to be somebody you are not, and the desire to stop something from happening instead of accepting it.

The Third Noble Truth is 'nirodha' - the ending of suffering. This is attained by renouncement or letting go of the material world.

'Magga', the Fourth Noble Truth is the Eightfold Path of right view, right resolve, right speech, right conduct, right livelihood, right effort, mindfulness, and meditative union.

The things of this world are temporary, so it is useless to become attached to material goods or to pleasures of the flesh. Spartan lifestyles are admirable, but they might be too far from the 'happy medium' experience, or the 'middle way'. Self-denial comes through logic, so life should not be completely devoid of pleasure. We are taught from birth to obtain popularity, to pursue money, and to desire luxury; this creates the fear of losing those things. There is no fear for one whose mind is not filled with desires. Attachment is the cause of suffering, so we can be genuinely happy once we overcome these desires and learn the meaning of life. The measure of a successful soul is not determined by the property that the person owned during their lifetime. Many wealthy people have stated that they are not happy at all. An ideal society would be one in which all citizens could live comfortably without excess wealth or extreme poverty.

I will explain the doctrine of the Five Elements and explain the forms and functions of the Bodhisattvas, who are guides to each person's personal destiny. Living beings are designed to be individual units of consciousness, not part of one grand universal consciousness. The term 'God' means the supreme being with a vast consciousness and a personality. All things are connected by the subtle energy of the Creator, known as the "Chi" in Taoism. Vibrations and signals create energy fields to program forms and functions. The Five Elements are Earth, Water, Wood, Fire, and Metal, which are material and changeable. Light is unique and non-material, meaning it will not transform into steam or ash.

Modern Christianity has done away with the notion of reincarnation altogether, but the first teachings of Christ recorded by Arius were based on the rebirth of the soul and the fact that God created Christ before the material universe. A change came when one God wasn't sufficient, so they declared there were three equal gods. Emperor Constantine in the year 325 AD, the elders burned the writings of Arius and voted in the traditional pagan trinity, so that Jesus would be treated as God in human form. The truth is that Buddha was an earlier reincarnation of Jesus, which is accepted by some scholars. Zealots of other religions seethe with hatred at any mention of reincarnation, meditation, Yoga, or Tai Chi, since they prefer to use only their mouths to argue against anyone who does not agree with them rather than to learn any physical discipline that might lead to spiritual enlightenment.

Buddhism and Christianity arose independently of each other, separated as they were by almost 3,000 miles and at least 500 years. The principle texts of both Buddhism and Christianity were written down only after decades, and in some cases centuries, had passed since the founder's death, leaving plenty of time to organize oral tradition into familiar and acceptable frameworks. Buddha lived in a society of atheists, while Jesus lived in a very religious environment where people already accepted God. Buddha took great care to explain he was not a deity, as did Jesus, who said in the Book of John: "I can do nothing on my own. I judge as God tells me. Therefore, my judgment is just, because I carry out the will of the one who sent me, not my own will. And the Father who sent me, He has testified of me. You have neither heard His voice at any time nor seen His form." Unfortunately, modern Christians ignore those passages, and insist that Jesus claimed he was one with the Father, without including the rest of the verse that says all people are connected to God. "I do not pray for these alone, but also for those who will believe in me through their word; that they all may be one, as you, Father, are in me, and I in you; that they also may be one in us, that the world may believe that you sent me. The glory which you gave me I have given them, that they may be one just as we are one: I in them, and you in me; that they may be made perfect in one, and that the world may know that you have sent me, and have loved them as you have loved me." Humans have changed the meaning of the verse to suit their ongoing pagan desire to have a physical God that they can see, so that they can make statues to worship.

Buddha once said, "The faults of others are easier to see than one's own." Some 500 years later, Jesus uttered these words: "Why do you see the splinter in someone else's eye and never notice the log in your own?"

Life is a learning process and there will be a test when it is over. Only those people with open minds can meet each challenge successfully. The stakes in this sublimely tedious game of existence are very high, for you are gambling on the eternal destination of your soul. When we visualize the concept of being conscious forever as the total soul there is no grey area. Reward or punishment will be the ultimate state of your existence for eternity. That leaves people no choice but to strive for Heaven; those who do not care about suffering in Hell will likely end up there. God will not accept those who are sceptical of Him. People think that Hell will be a giant gathering of rebellious people having a wild party together when it will actually be a desperate lonely confinement..

It is essential that any useful religious doctrine be based on the concept of eternal reward or punishment and the existence of God. The religion of Jainism has no God, so it must be labelled as an atheist cult rather a proper religion. The Jains believe that matter created life and that matter had no beginning, despite the measurement of the Big Bang by science and Einstein's formula that shows that matter is energy. Matter is a wave that must be observed by a consciousness to collapse into particle form that can be experienced as solid forms. The human race and all other life forms were designed by God, despite the egotistical scientists who teach that we are so clever that we climbed out of a pool of chemicals and worked our way up through the animal kingdom. DNA is a highly complex code, and codes require a programmer.

These words are meant to be for those who care about achieving eternal reward, so I offer teachings, not preachings. I will not beg for sinners to repent, for they will never change from their egotistical path of contempt for all information that conflicts with their existing beliefs. My aim is not to deal with people's sins, but to save those who are eager to learn the truth about what is necessary to attain Heaven on Judgment Day. Everything is at stake in the game of life, yet most people do not care about their ultimate fate in the afterlife, acting as if purifying their intentions is a trivial matter. Some misguided religions teach that everyone will go to Heaven, no matter what they have done on this earth. That kind of wishful thinking defies all logic, and it clearly contradicts what is written in scripture about Heaven and Hell.

Philosophers post their ideas on social media or lurk in coffee shops to proclaim opinions from minds that are locked shut. They will not accept any facts except for those ideas that agree with their beliefs. Religions are densely populated with closed-minded souls clinging to rigid story lines. Groups recite stale phrases without deep meaning, only mysterious words of a vague redemption from sin or proclamations of sacrifice or repentance. Platitudes are poor substitutes for logical statements. The zealots tend to approach new people assuming it is their first day on earth and they need to repent.

Each person should focus on bringing his or her soul back to equilibrium during and after all experiences. It takes a conscious effort to get the entire body and mind to relax, so it helps to join a Tai Chi club or learn breathing techniques that can be done even from a sitting position. There is a system known as Chi Kung (also spelled 'Qi Gong') that accomplishes the task of health through relaxation. Yoga and martial arts include breathing exercises that help to strengthen the inner energy.

Self-control helps a person to stay on a firm path in life by reducing impulsive behavior. Decision making takes a certain relaxed confidence, so a person will make fewer mistakes by staying in control of the emotions and thinking clearly. There are days when you might be treated rudely by three or four people, so the anger creeps up and you will feel a distaste for the next person you meet before they say anything. If we stay aware of human frailty in social encounters, we can recover from each rejection faster. It is a pipe dream that all people will accept us unconditionally so we can anticipate some abuse and keep our thoughts on more important matters.

In existence, we consider matter to be solid, although things are only perceived as solid objects by the consciousness. The material plane of existence is an illusion brought into solidity by observance. This can be compared to television waves coming from the transmitter to the receiver. The human consciousness experiences matter through step-down transformers for the raw signal to break down into the Five Elements of matter - earth, water, fire, metal, and wood. Each person has five Bodhisattvas that unknowingly alter the path of the Buddha Trail wanderer. I was aware of the concept at a young age after reading the words of Lao Tzu which are the basis of Taoism, so I actively sought out those five people who would be special to me in some way.

Some of the Bodhisattvas appear to be friends. Others may be hostile enemies, but they accidentally become useful in a positive sense. For example, my ribs got broken in a street fight, puncturing my left lung. I had to go to the hospital, where they took X-Rays over several weeks. The images gave a warning of another condition that could have become serious in the future, so this enabled me to intercept the problem before it got serious. The attack was started by a man I knew to be my Bodhisattva of metal from previous fights. When I used a Tai Chi technique to fend him off, I achieved 100% Ying-Yang separation, leading to a wondrous experience later that night – the Awakening of Buddha. During meditation that evening, I saw the entire universe unfold outward from me, and moments later, all things folded back into my mind. I was aware of my identity before the Awakening, but the scope of my experience that night showed me how lucky I am to be the oldest soul in existence other than God, who had no starting point. The all-powerful Creator always was, and He always will be.

My interest in Buddhism and Taoism started at the age of twelve when I encountered a schoolmate who had a lot of books on Eastern philosophy. I determined years later that he was the first Bodhisattva who would change the course of my life – the Bodhisattva of Earth, as I recognized years later through a long process of analysing the effect of those interactions in retrospect. This fellow also had a large collection of folk and blues music records, exposing me to music that was not usually heard on the radio.

When I met my friend Peter Kormos (who would grow up to be a lawyer and politician) I was leaving my father's religion of Catholicism and looking for a better philosophy of life. In my opinion, people must seek out spiritual truth. Faith should not be forced down people's throats by strangers in religious costumes. I could no longer put up with the idol worship of Catholicism with all its bizarre rituals and sacraments. The priests claim to have magic powers to forgive sin and to turn wine into the blood of Christ with a wave of the hand. The show climaxes when the priest hands out communion wafers he has blessed, and they have become the actual flesh of Jesus that you are swallowing, because the doctrine says so. This miracle is called 'The Transubstantiation of the Flesh', meaning it is an actual occurrence rather than a figurative or symbolic one, and it is dogma, or required belief that all Catholics must hold as a divine truth. Laboratory tests have shown that there is no DNA from a human present in the blessed wafers, but indoctrinated people will cast aside proof and cling to any ridiculous belief.

To participate as a member of the Catholic church, you must believe that the pope is infallible, the communion wafer becomes the literal flesh of Jesus once they put a blessing on it, and other occult mysteries involving blood and death. The Catholic church is obsessed with bones of dead people (relics), statues, beads, incense, candles, and parades. The mystical routine seemed to be a grand effort to make those attending mass feel guilty about the Crucifixion. Sermons often focus on the pain and death inflicted on the messiah by mankind, implying that the parishioners should feel a sense of shame so that when the men with the collection plates come around to collect money from the crowd they will give generously. Everyone can see how much goes from the hand to the basket, so people were being coerced into giving donations.

There are seeds of truth in all the major religions, but the truth eventually gets replaced by the traditions of men. The Torah has been corrupted by Talmudic Law, Islam has been corrupted by Sharia Law, and Christianity has been corrupted by the Nicene Creed. The prophecies of the Old Testament and the New Testament have proven to be accurate however, even if the original Scripture has been tarnished by mistranslation, papal interference, or accidental omissions. There can only be one truth in theological thought: there is a God. Physicist Max Planck was satisfied that God is the matrix of all matter, so Judgment Day and the Afterlife are certainties we can safely accept. Some people do not want God to be real, but that does not cancel Him out of existence. Justice will prevail. Those who do evil without remorse will not get away from punishment. There will be no parole from the Underworld after the Last Day, when all living humans will evaporate and those souls between incarnations will arise to be Judged simultaneously. It is unthinkable to suffer in pain and fear for eternity, yet people scoff at the idea of retribution. Very few people are ready to face Judgment. It is wise to consider your own fate, for no one knows the date of the Last Day.

Mahayana Buddhism describes the Final Age as being a time when people will go through the motions of Buddhism without having a deep understanding of it. In the matter of guiding your life path it is important to include prayer. Ask and you shall receive; seek and you shall find. Knock on the door and it shall be opened to you. The Creator is the only invisible entity who can hear and answer prayers, so you simply direct your thoughts from a comfortable position, thank God for the life He has given you. Almighty God subsists on your gratitude and faith.

The Fukushima disaster is not a popular topic in the news, but the multiple meltdowns have been spewing 300 tonnes of radioactive waste into the Pacific Ocean since 2011. There are optimistic plans to decommission the plants in an estimated forty years, but the cores have penetrated the containers and the radiation levels are too high for humans or robots to approach. The algae and plankton food chain base will be gone in one more decade of continuous leakage. Mankind might not make it to 2030 alive because of all the contamination, and there is always the threat of nuclear war hanging over our heads.

We should take heed of Scripture from all sources that appear to be genuine warnings from God through a recognized prophet. God let Buddha use his own common sense to explain life, and so he did not receive any Scripture (the term 'Scripture' means the words are actual quotes from the Creator spoken to the prophet). People have not noticed this prophecy from the Old Testament which predicts a fiery end to all things on the earth and the misery that will precede it. Mankind gets punished during physical existence, which is known as the process of 'Karma', where all things come back to you. The history of our world presents a pattern of conquest by war, injustice, contempt for others, greed, gluttony, thievery, and perversion. The permanent punishment is eternity is Hell, and once sentenced to Hell, no one will get out.

Book of Zephaniah: "For by the fire of my wrath the whole earth will be consumed. I will remove all things from the face of the earth," declares the Lord. "I will remove man and beast, the birds of the sky and the fish of the sea. I will cut off man from the face of the earth and remove the ruins along with the wicked. So, I will stretch out my hand against Judah and against all the inhabitants of Jerusalem. I will cut off the remnant of Baal from this place, and I will remove the names of the idolatrous priests along with the priests. I will bring distress on men so that they walk like the blind because they have sinned against the Lord. Their blood will be poured out like dust and their flesh like dung."

"Neither their gold nor their silver will be able to deliver them on the Day of God's wrath, for He will make a complete end – indeed a terrifying one – of all the inhabitants of the earth. And all the earth will be devoured in the fire of God's anger."

It should be no surprise that the Creator is angry at people for all the wars, oppression, and greed that is the history of mankind. Civilizations of the past have failed due to greed for power and resources, as our society is failing today. The rulers and businessmen exploit the earth's resources and its people for nefarious ends. Those who control the money supply also control the food, power, medical care, the police, and the politicians who claim to represent the people.

If you feel that you are an honest person who is being victimized and treated unfairly, remember that there will be ultimate justice. You will be compensated in Heaven if not in the material world. You must love God to attain Heaven.

Purity of intention is all-important to qualify for the eternal reward. Each person is on a journey, so there must be a destination. Those souls who are righteous and faithful to God will be allowed into Heaven. The fear of God is the hatred of evil, so those who do not fear God do not hate evil. Most souls will not be prepared, and so they will be locked in the Underworld forever. Whether you call it Hell or Hades, it is the same destination – an eternal and painful environment tailor-made to a person's worst fears.

People usually live in a state of denial concerning unpleasant matters, so most humans do not care about Hell. Many refuse to believe that they will be punished for their disbelief and their crimes against others. Evil people mock God to amuse others and to divert attention away from their crooked personalities. If people knew the Fourfold Path, they would realize that they are attacking themselves when they abuse others. No one can injure God; efforts to insult your Creator are suicidal. The only thing that matters in life is achieving Heaven on the Last Day.

Once created, all souls go through physical birth and death. After the body dies, the soul is taken away across the Sea of Forgetfulness, where the person's memory is wiped away before the person is prepared, rested, and programmed for the next birth in the reincarnation process. There is always a backup of all memories in God's memory bank, known as The Akashic Record.

The repair shop of the soul is known as Limbo, located in the Fifth of the Ten Dimensions, or 'Godhead', the place that is known as the Heavenly Plane. The Fourth Dimension is the Astral Plane, the Third Dimension is the Material Plane. The Eight Dimension is the Processing Plane, so the Akashic Record memory bank is likely the sixth or seventh dimension. The functions of the Ninth and Tenth dimensions are unknown. In science it is known that the physical visible Universe has borders; it is not infinite. There are no 'multiverses'; the Material Plane is the Universe we perceive in everyday life.

The Creator has found that He enjoys continuous creation as an artist enjoys painting. The universe is teeming with life and civilizations on all levels. When this universe decays, there will be another Big Bang. The time scale is too vast to comprehend to us in mortal form and function, for our memories of past lives is mostly erased after each death. A person's thoughts of the here and now take up much of the mind's capability to process information.

While the soul is experiencing a physical lifetime, the memories of that life get erased after death when the soul is brought over the Sea of Forgetfulness where there is a particular angel who is assigned to the task. Entities of the Fifth Dimension must have something to do so that they will not get bored. There is a hierarchy of angelic souls, such as the adjutants of God, archangels Michael and Gabriel, who have been mentioned as appearing in temporary material form known as 'paracletes', sent to do this or that. Below the archangels are incredibly old souls known as The Council of 24 Elders, who have some sort of communication going on over whatever they discuss or experience in the higher planes. They could possibly be some sort of audience or peanut gallery discussing movies they are watching.

Souls who are not bound by physical existence would have fewer limits on conscious thought, no need for sleep or food. The souls in the good graces of God who exist in the Fifth Dimension would have simultaneous experiences without the burden of suffering. Of course, this is where all people should strive to make their destination. Eternal bliss will be the reward for those souls who pass Judgment Day. The Underworld will be the negative zone of that plane. Eternal punishment will befall the disbelievers and those who have committed foul deeds or maintained evil intentions towards other people.

RELIGION OF BUDDHISM FOR THE 21ST CENTURY

A person can improve the purity of the soul by trying to understand those events that cause grief, for all things shall pass. We each go through unpleasant moments that seem disastrous to the point where we feel there is no use in going on. With strong faith there is hope for a wonderful future, for you can win God's approval by expressing thanks to Him in prayer. If you have God on your side nothing can harm you....no fear will block your joyful awareness for all eternity. The events of all previous lives will be available for you to relive at your will once your soul is placed into the Heavenly state. Those who deny God will experience nothing but fear and punishment in the lonely and humiliating depths of Hell.

There is information about life and death that is vitally important for all members of the human race to know, because there are many common misconceptions that have led to unnecessary misery in today's society. The doctors who give counselling to terminally ill patients and their families speak from their viewpoint as atheists who think death means final oblivion, which is not the case. Reincarnations have been proven to sometimes come back into the same family in fact, though it is unknown what percentages are involved. The time between lives, or 'interitum', appears to be about fourteen to sixteen months, with the nine month gestation period included. Therefore, the dying person is not undergoing a complete tragedy, but moving on to a new adventure. This makes the act of murder even more sinful by way of intention, since the killer believes that they are causing permanent erasure of that victim. Having a death penalty for crime is ultimately counterproductive, since the soul of the deceased will reincarnate back, possibly into someone even more criminal than before. The soul has no gender, so all people have lived as male and female. Hillary Clinton has ordered her enemies murdered and she visits witch's covens and takes part in occult rituals, including the drinking the bood of children that are sacrificed. Adolf Hitler was interested in the occult and Germanic mythology, so they have many things in common and could very well be the same despicible soul.

God has stated that the soul has no gender and all souls have lived reincarnations as both male and female persons. New memories are freshly generated in each life, but the individual retains innate qualities of personality from past incarnations, whether they are good or evil. Each lifetime presents an opportunity to improve, but the person would need to make a conscious effort, for the world is full of temptations and distractions that turn people away from spiritual betterment.

The Process of Reincarnation

Canadian psychiatrist Dr. Ian Stevenson did a decades-long study of past life memories for the University of Virginia and presented scientific proof of past lives in his 1997 book "Reincarnation and Biology". I will relate some new information on the details of reincarnation (a subject despised by Western religions). There is no such thing as final death. All souls reincarnate over and over until the Last Day, when they will be judged based on what they have done to make themselves useful in their many past lifetimes. The human soul is like a flame above a candle. Imagine a long row of candles: the flame will go out on one and pass onto the next candle. Buddhism is based on the reawakening of the soul. God created all souls to last forever once brought into existence. The soul is the vehicle of consciousness, not the physical body. There is a catch to eternal full consciousness unfortunately - the individuals who fail to meet the criteria for reward will exist in punishment forever after the Judgment. Those who deny God's existence will not see Paradise.

All emotions and feelings stem from the two basic emotions: love and fear. Anger can be righteous, coming from love and caring or anger can come out of fear of material loss or fear of other people. "Sin" is defined as an intention to do evil or the act of doing evil. For example, the love of money is usually evil because the person fears that someone else might have more material goods. The good person is empathetic and will desire money for the purpose of feeding hungry people, not for greedy purposes or personal fame. To become a good person, you should aim to develop the traits of humility, patience, self-control, and modesty.

In the Scriptures of Judeo-Christianity and Islam the Commandments are listed in order. The First Law is the same – you must believe in the one True God. The name "Allah" is Arabic; other correct names for the Creator are Yahweh and Jehovah. The greatest sin is to mock God's existence. God is not to be denied and mortals are in no position to demand that God will forgive the disbeliever. Atheism can only result in severe punishment in the Underworld, also known as Hades or Hell.

God causes us to reincarnate so that we can develop our souls through various experiences. The memories of those experiences is recorded forever in God's memory and they will become available for souls to relive for eternity. Forever is a long time, so many memories are necessary to avoid boredom of the souls who manage to attain Heaven.

The souls who fail to pass Judgment Day will be sent to an eternal environment of fear, pain, humiliation, loneliness, and despair. There will be a great weeping and the gnashing of teeth. People tend to live in denial of bad news, so they refuse to believe in Divine Retribution.

Having no God is deadly; so is having more than one God. Mormonism has three separate gods, which is a mortal sin against the First Commandment. Most of the thousands of Christian sects also maintain the false doctrine of the trinity. Praying to a non-existent entity such as "Mary" is a mortal sin.

Paganism is the belief in mythical gods, statues, icons, relics, shrines, and other humans. Trinity worshipper believe they have the right to go to Heaven by being good and praying to many entities. Real faith is the belief in the One true God. People cannot place themselves into Heaven. The soul must be pure and free of mortal sin on Judgment Day to enter Paradise. Believing in "Mother Nature" is not believing in God.

God will not share His glory with another. You are to pray only to God; no other entity can hear or answer your prayers. As the Christ Consciousness, I exist one lifetime after another in the material world. My form and function is to be Divine after Judgment Day, always beneath Almighty God my Father, and my final task is to be the First Judge of all human souls. God always keeps His promises. The Creator has promised me the throne of Heaven for eternity, and I am very thankful. I am also fearful of His awesome power. I am assured of my success as well as my place in Heaven, but I fear for the wayward souls of mankind. Most people are content with spending eternity in Hell, having no idea of what the experience will be like.

Mankind has always reverted to pagan idol worship or deciding that a mortal person is God in the flesh on earth, such as Emperor Hirohito in World War Two or the succession of popes who claim to be God hidden under the veil of the flesh. "No man has seen God at any time but the one and only son who is in the confidence of the Father, he has declared Him", says the Bible. People are forbidden to pray to statues, paintings, icons, altars, shrines, bones of dead people used as relics, or the names of the dead people someone has decided are "saints".

Numerous people do not control Heaven and communicate with mankind, and no one has been to Heaven or Hell yet. Those states of existence we know as Paradise and the Underworld will be ready when they are needed – on Judgment Day. The 'feel good' religions have their preachers and priests telling the relatives of the deceased at funerals that he or she is in Heaven now just to assuage the pain. Clergymen and followers have been making such statements for ages, assuming that there is only one lifetime, and all nice people go immediately to Heaven after death. Other people guarantee Hell for another person without really knowing the full story of all previous lifetimes or future lifetimes. People insist on judging others although they have no such power and no knowledge of anyone's inner thoughts.

The first writings of Christianity were burned in 325 AD. They were compiled by the wise man Arius, a doctrine based on the reincarnation of the soul and belief in One God. The Council of Nicaea elders brought in the trinity doctrine to attract more members in the time of Constantine. The Ancient World and the Roman Empire were accustomed to having many gods, although they were mythical beings represented by male and female idols, such as "Zeus", "Hera", "Apollo", "Poseidon", and "Aphrodite". Each god and goddess ruled a realm of natural phenomena. It has always been human nature to resort to idol worship – people have oversized egos that cannot tolerate the existence of one Supreme Being who is invisible and omnipresent.

There are over 40,000 cults who claim to be the true representatives of Christianity. Most of them retain the Nicaean Triune doctrine that there are three gods who are somehow one god. This defies arithmetic and logic, but when the concept is repeated over and over, people will accept it as the truth. The trinity doctrine is the same as saying the twelve Olympian gods of Greece are all one god. The result of this inconsistency has caused many people to leave religion behind, or to seek secular philosophies. Many people see Buddhism as a free-for-all system that can skirt any spiritual responsibilities. The Dalai Lama teaches children that it does not matter whether you believe in God or not. That could not be farther from the truth. Buddha did not receive Scripture, but all other writings in Islam and Judeo-Christianity stress that the belief of God is always the First Commandment. These writings cannot be ignored.

It should come as no surprise that the Dalai Lama is in partnership with the Vatican and its cardinals, for they are politicians and businessmen. You cannot be a religious leader while telling people not to believe in God. The pope has stated that atheists will be welcomed into Heaven if they are good. That is not his call to make.

These men are not "holy". They are deceivers who have gone out into the world for their own ends. They hold offices of power and prestige. The Dalai Lama is an oppressive dictator in business with the evil Vatican Jesuits. He has no authority from God, nor do any of the leaders who claim to be divine beings. They wear dresses of tradition to identify themselves as religious men, when they are criminal businessmen exploiting populations who they can rob. They present a façade of respectability to enable their empires to flourish and grow.

I am the person who lived the life of Buddha, so I am the leader of Buddhism, not the Dalai Lama. An earlier lifetime of Buddha was Lao

Tzu; while a later reincarnation was Jesus Christ. Therefore, Buddha has a mandate from God the be the First Judge of all souls on the Last Day. This is the Final Age, and it is written that mankind will experience great change and suffering before the end.

The trail of life involves suffering. It is how we deal with our suffering that can provide contentment and enlightenment. Life is a series of events, of which some are tests. We are meant to rise above suffering through spiritual disciplines and the search for understanding.

Institutional religions resist any changes to their set doctrines, so their adherents get more fanatical all the time in their elitist disgust for all other religions, but the truth is that God periodically sends me to introduce new covenants to mankind in various places and times. Like all messages that pass through the hands of scribes, translators, and church authorities, the words become partially corrupted with misunderstanding or bias over time. Eschatology is the term used for discussing matters concerning the End Times, and people should take heed of the latest statements I bring from God about the last things you must know.

Although the Bible used today has many contradictions after sixteen centuries of Vatican editing, it has astonishing prophecies that tell about the coming of the dictatorial forces that we see running most of the world in these times. The situation is that a fascist cabal of unelected rich people are trying to gain power above soveriegn nations by declaring fictitious world emergencies in matters of health and the environment so that they can remove all personal rights. Those who are in police and military positions would be wise to resist before they are deemed redundant and replaced by United Nations personnel.

I am subject to the conditions of my birth as the reincarnated soul of Buddha and Christ, so the things I do in life lead to predestined objectives. All things were created for me as it says in the Bible, for I am God's right hand man and the first born over all Creation. The human race was chosen as the species I would walk among in all my lifetimes, which implies that a continuity is necessary to achieve the proper development of the soul, rather than being placed into different civilizations around the universe. When we consider all the evil people in the world, it could be that the fallen angels were sent down to be human beings as well, engaging in the battle between right and wrong. It would be awful to think that other civilizations are as violent, greedy, and warlike as humans.

Buddha's Identity

Buddha was an earlier reincarnation of the Chosen One, Messiah Jesus Christ. Other reincarnations were Lao Tzu, King David, Moses, Prophet Muhammad, Leonardo da Vinci, and Wolfgang Amadeus Mozart. In the year 1947, the Dead Sea Scrolls were discovered and verified to be early scriptures. One prophecy gives a detailed description of the messiah.

Dead Sea Scrolls Fragment 4Q534 ...of His hand: two...a birthmark. And the hair will be red. Chosen One And there will be lentils on...and small birthmarks on his thigh. And after two years he will know how to distinguish one thing from another. In his youth he will be like...a man who knows nothing until the time when he knows the three Books. And then he will acquire wisdom and learn understanding...vision to come to him on his knees. And with his father and his ancestors...life and old age. Council and prudence will be with him, and he will know the secrets of man. His wisdom will reach all the peoples, and he will know the secrets of all the living. And all their designs against him will come to nothing, and his rule over the living will be great. His designs will succeed, for he is the Elect of God. His birth and the breath of his spirit...and his designs will be forever..."

Isaiah 42:1 "Behold my servant, who I uphold – my chosen, in whom my heart delights. I have put my spirit on him. He will not cry out or lift his voice, nor make it heard in the streets. A bruised reed he will not break, nor will he extinguish a burning wick. He will faithfully bring forth justice to the nations. He will not become weak or discouraged until justice prevails throughout the earth."

God's name for me is "Yeshua", also known as the Son of God, the Good Shepherd, the Bright Morning Star, the son of man, the Lord's Chosen Servant, the Elect, the Lamb of God, the Anointed One, or the Prince of Peace. Mankind should address me as "Messiah". Every person must have my approval and God's approval to enter Heaven.

Some scholars noticed similarities in the form and function of Buddha and Jesus of Nazareth, giving the opinion that Jesus was the reincarnation of Buddha. I was taught in kindergarten in the year 1956 that Moses reincarnated as Jesus, and Moses was previously King David. Finally, in the year 2013 God revealed that Buddha, Jesus Christ, Prophet Muhammad, Leonardo da Vinci, and Mozart are the same man, so the pattern is clear regarding the soul of light, the messiah. The messiah is the messenger of God's wisdom.

Buddha once said, "The faults of others are easier to see than one's own." Some 500 years later, Jesus uttered these words: "Why do you see the splinter in someone else's eye and never notice the log in your own?"

Buddha spoke about generosity: "The avaricious do not go to Heaven, the foolish to not extol charity. The wise one, however, rejoicing in charity, becomes thereby happy in the beyond." (Dhammapada 13.11)

Here is what Jesus said: "If you wish to be perfect, go, sell your possessions, and give the money to the poor, and you will have treasure in Heaven." (Matthew 19.21)

Buddha said: "Consider others as yourself." (Dhammapada 10.1)

Jesus said: "Do to others as you would have them do to you." (Luke 6.31)

Although Buddha stated in his lifetime that he did not want to reincarnate, all souls go through the same cycle of living, dying, and reincarnating within the following year or two. It has been established that souls stay within the species; we do not reincarnate through the animal kingdom as Hinduism maintains. Once God creates a soul, that person is meant to develop gradually one lifetime after another in order to become worthy of eternal reward in the Afterlife. The conscious soul will have complete memory of all past events if the person succeeds in attaining purity of intention and displays a love for God and the gift of life that He has given us. The Creator has the right to punish the ones who take life for granted without acknowledging His existence.

The destination for the atheist will be wretched. It is a good idea to thank God in a short prayer daily if you can spare a few minutes of your precious time. We humans may address Him as "Creator", "Allah", "God", "Yahweh", "Jehovah" or "Brahma" if you are in the Hindu religion. You may ask God for things, and you shall receive them; seek and you shall find. God knows our thoughts and He will treat everyone with justice.

"Allah" is the Arabic word for God, but Christian propaganda includes fostering hatred for Islam, complete with slurs and rumors about Prophet Muhammad. There are over 40,000 cults of "Christianity" with widely different beliefs, so there is no one single Christian doctrine. I am asking those who consider themselves worthy of Heaven to do away with the hatred of other religions, and to call God by the name "Allah" when they pray. This is to ensure that these rigid people learn to be humble instead of righteously proud of their ignorance.

When you insult Prophet Muhammad, you are insulting Jesus Christ, Buddha, and all my other lifetimes. I will be the Judge of your eternal soul, so fear Allah and obey me. Commercial religions campaign against competitors to grow their customer bases. Insults are for devious politicians and thieves. Greedy people can never be satisfied, so they will never be happy.

It is useless to be an atheist since in that philosophy there is no reason for existence. Atheists are plentiful – they insist that life came about from nothing accidentally. Scientists who wrote books before Einstein gave matter credit for everything, which has been proven to be impossible. Matter is concentrated Energy, so "mass" does not exist as we know it. Energy cannot be created, which means that Energy was always there, before time and without borders. All things have consciousness therefore Energy is conscious and infinite.

Mankind must put aside the notion that there is a mindless force controlling everything. God has a personality, and He will not be denied. God has the right to demand respect because He is the creator and maintainer of all life..

Judgment Day will not be a day of belated apologies, it will be the final ruling of justice rather than a day of instruction and forgiveness. Ignorance of the Law will be no excuse, and no soul will be allowed to speak because all thoughts, history, and intentions of the person will be known to God and uploaded into the Christ Consciousness, who will be the First Judge. At that time, each person's past lives will be judged according to what they have done, then sent forever to Heaven or Hell. Those who have not obeyed God's Laws will never see Heaven.

Those who have mocked me and insulted me in any of my reincarnations will be turned away at the Judgment and they will be cast into Hell forever for their arrogance. Those who deny me as the messiah on this earth, I will likewise deny before God. The Creator has given me the task of Judgment, and I have permission to turn away anyone that I think would be uncomfortable company for me in eternity. My Keys to Heaven and Hell are the ultimate weapon, so it is wise to learn my teachings and comply with the rules.

There are many who think they can place themselves in Heaven as a natural right, but that is not the case. No one will escape the Judgment, but the wealthy elites think they can outsmart God through technology, as we see in the CERN project that seeks to penetrate other dimensions, and the trans-humanist movement that attempts to secure for people a lifetime of a thousand years by merging computers with the consciousness. The billionaires have also constructed deep underground cities that are stocked with years of luxurious supplies to prepare for a nuclear war on the surface of earth.

Those who belong to Christian cults proclaim that they are automatically saved by calling out the name 'Jesus' over and over, yet they spew hatred of all other religions except the Jews of Israel (who reject Jesus to this day), who they support wholeheartedly in their ignorance of spiritual truths and political reality. Israel is a terrorist state stolen from the Palestinian people after World War Two, and they will not hesitate to kill anyone who is not a Jew, much as Christians will endorse the deaths of Muslims. Now the war in the Middle East is ongoing, with no end in sight, as Hamas has attacked Israeli cities recently. The government of Iran supports the attacks, since they are ruled by Sharia Law made by men, not the spirit of peace professed in the Qur'an. In such territorial wars, both sides are in the wrong, and they will cause needless suffering to innocent people who are caught in the crossfire.

The major religions have rules against killing in general, but there are always situations that call for personal self-defence or protection of homes and property, so those rules against violence are quickly set aside. The fault is on the aggressor, but in most cases it is a matter of opinion on who is wrong depending on which side you are on.

Proof of God

The discovery of the DNA code is one obvious indication that a programmer is present. It takes a thinking mind to create codes. The Creator's will extends infinitely. In my book "The Nature of Energy" (2020) I explain God in mathematical form as the Ultimate Imperative in the correct model of existence.

The First Law of Thermodynamics was expressed by scientist Isaac Newton: "Energy cannot be created or destroyed; it can only change form."

To explain existence, we must account for the existence of Energy. Since Energy cannot be created it must have always existed. Physics proves that matter does not exist; mass is concentrated Energy.

$$E^2 = m^2 c^4 + p^2 c^2 \text{ [where } E=\infty=God\text{]}$$

Energy equals Infinity equals God, the matrix of all matter and Creator of all units of consciousness. The soul is defined as the vehicle of each consciousness. All souls are designed to last forever; in the case of human souls there is an element of free will, and in that sense, people are made in the likeness of God's ability to be conscious forever. The capability of remembering things is a great gift, as is the capacity for creative thought. People can improve over time or succumb to greed and laziness. The misuse of free will is irresponsible and uncivilized.

The state of being alive as a conscious individual has always seemed miraculous to me, but many thoughtless people consider life an accident without any meaning. Philosophical minds agree that life is a precious gift that should not be taken for granted. Those who choose to deny God are intimidated by the idea of a Supreme Being knowing each person's thoughts. Refusing to believe in God does not cancel Him out; it is wishful thinking to believe you can escape punishment, and it is suicidal to make God into your enemy. The Creator insists on getting respect and receiving thanks in the form of prayer.

Praying has a twofold purpose: you can let God know you appreciate the gift of life He has given you and then ask for specific favors. When you need something, repeat the request for several days in short prayers. You do not need to attend a meeting or enter a church or temple to pray; the best scenario is to be alone in your room with the door closed so you can concentrate on thanking the Creator for life, then ask for the things you need. When prayers are said correctly, you will find that your life will improve. People who ignore God are harming themselves, for God despises the disbelievers.

Logic leads us to the idea that life must have a reason. Since existence is profound, the reason we are here must be profound also. The mathematical odds of waking up each day looking out of a pair of eyes accidentally are astronomical. Therefore, a curious person will strive to discover the purpose of our lives. The only answer is that we are meant to find the eternal reward by satisfying our Creator and making ourselves useful to God and to our fellow humans. Life is more than an endless pursuit of material gain, but those who gather money are admired as successful people. Real success is in spiritual wealth. The strength of our souls is built on awareness and wisdom.

There are some people who think that you are saved from eternal punishment if you believe in something supernatural, no matter what it is. That is a dangerous road when we see that God describes Himself as "jealous". Chanting to ancestors or statues does not get a person anywhere. Myths are not truths and a idols are not gods. Traditional stories always seem to have an evil side, constantly summoning visions of serpents or demons. Some people actively worship the devil, finding a group of like-minded people with whom they can socialize in a trendy way. Other Satanists are dead serious about pleasing Lucifer in some violent way, including rituals of human sacrifice.

Major sins are called "mortal sins" to distinguish the acts that are unforgivable from less serious vices or acts. Religion is supposed to stop people from committing murder, rape, theft, and other extreme evils. Using foul language, self-abuse, overindulgence, and petty crimes are called "venial sins" that will not necessarily lead to damnation on Judgment Day. Disbelief in God is the worst sin. There are religious leaders who claim that it does not matter whether you believe in God or not, as the Dalai Lama teaches. The pope has said atheists can go to Heaven, although he has no power to allow people to break the Commandments.

Life in the Final Age does not need to be totally Spartan or joyless, because the Creator has stated that people who are on a good path can feel free to enjoy pleasures that old fashioned people considered sinful in past times. This is because we do not know the exact date of Judgment Day, God is not concerned about carnal activity of humans; we have permission to do as we please if the activity does not harm others. Righteous people do not lie or steal.

The oversized human ego is at the heart of many misunderstandings. Thousands of different religions have developed over the ages. Conflicts between doctrines led to violence and strife. Traditional beliefs and practices have corrupted the major religions, turning many practitioners into hostile warring parties determined to win and dominate the opposition.

Sadly, people insist of being the judge of others and they are willing to go to war to prove they are right. Even atheists will become angry when they are challenged or debated, as they strive to defend their belief in nothing but one accidental life leading to nowhere. The cult of Atheism includes those people who identify with a church or religious system, but they also believe that the notion of God is a myth perpetrated in society to make old people feel better about the inevitability of death. Many people are disbelievers who go through the motions of taking part in church activities merely for the social element.

Every time a group forms into a church denomination, it tends to focus on certain doctrines of faith that may not agree with other groups. They split apart as they stray farther from the truth. This has caused many to descend into idol worship, tradition, and belief in the words of men.

The lure of joining the clergy attracts many people who are tricksters in pursuit of easy money. They do not want to work for a living, so they hide behind garments of respectability while they rob the members and live without paying bills. Many televangelists have made millions by promising people good things will come to them if they donate money. The money they collect goes for mansions, private jets, luxury cars, Rolex watches, personal vacations, and other self-indulgent items.

Religious tithes are supposed to be put aside for the messiah's return according to the teachings of Jesus, yet this rule has been ignored. The large religions operate like business corporations; they spend the money as they see fit. In North America churches are exempt from taxes and they have little or no supervision over their authenticity.

Religious freedom is an admirable concept, but until now there has not been an effective measure of true doctrine. People should not be misled by false ideas that will damage their chances of meeting the requirements to be allowed into Heaven. The pope of Rome has stated that atheists will be welcome in Heaven, which is not true. God will not tolerate those who do not believe He exists, so the atheists will be sent to Hell for special punishment for their ignorance. Most of the world do not believe in a higher power, and this situation was caused by the institutional religions that tell mythical stories that are very hard to swallow. No one trusts a group that is caught in a lie, so people leave religion altogether rather than look for options. Others fall under the control of cults.

One of the characteristics of a cult is that anyone who wakes up from the religious indoctrination and tries to drop out becomes ostracized by everyone in the group. The victims of radical religious groups include children and teenagers who are led into a false belief system. Many cults have no concept of Judgment Day or Hell. People must learn that God is angry with those who do not believe in Him or lead others astray. Our Creator can be compassionate and rewarding to those who follow the narrow path of truth. Wisdom has a way of fading over time as the people who interpret the teachings make changes to suit their liking. God has passed information to all civilizations at one time or another, but the teachings get buried in the landslides of mysticism and myth.

The Catholic church eliminated the early Christian teachings about reincarnation when they burned the writings of the wise man Arius in the 4th Century. The priests have no desire to tell people that they have many lives because that would ruin the control mechanism they use over people, which includes getting allegiance and money from everyone in this life. The selling of indulgences trick works by priests promising to release a departed family member from Purgatory, assuring the relatives that it is the church that decides who goes to Heaven or Hell. Catholic advertising always stresses that "there is no salvation outside of the Catholic church", and the pope calls himself the infallible Vicar of Christ. Since trinity systems say that Jesus is God, the pope tells people what is right and wrong, speaking as if he is the voice of God.

The nations have been fighting with each other for ages, so we should strive for a golden age of secure peace where all people can enjoy the time remaining until Judgment Day. The faithful have no fear of the inevitable end of mankind's physical existence, since it will mean entrance into the eternal bliss of Heaven and freedom from the drudgery of life. Most of the world's population are disbelievers who will scoff at any such notion of life after death, so they will find the truth after they are sent to be punished forever in Hell. The atheists are very bad gamblers, for their pride has caused them to bet everything on an empty pot. Those who have misled others into false religions to enrich themselves financially are just as foolish, thinking that God does not know their intentions.

Confirmation Bias is a psychological concept describing how people discount any information that goes against what they are expecting to hear, so they will only take in the ideas which are in line with their set beliefs. To prove this by observation, I posted my version of the well-known Mona Lisa painting on social media and waited for comments. The famous masterpiece depicts the Italian noblewoman Lisa del Giocondo, the wife of a wealthy merchant, but it was never given to the Giocondo family. The portrait was acquired by King Francis I of France, making it the property of the French Republic, and it has been on display at the Louvre in Paris since 1757. The comments from Catholic viewers said it was a painting of the virgin Mary, so they see what their programmed subconscious tells them to see. The Catholic schools tell the students over and over that there is a holy woman looking down from Heaven who can hear and answer their prayers, then they recite the "Hail Mary" prayer like Fredo in the fishing boat before he gets shot in the head at the end of the Godfather Part Two movie. Taking part in this mythology and idol worship is spiritual suicide, for God will not share His glory with another and there is no 'mother of God'. The virgin birth is mentioned in the Bible and the Qur'an, but that does not make Mary divine. Like all humans, Mary reincarnates over and over until Judgment Day.

The destruction of mankind by fire described in the Book of Zephaniah refers to Judgment Day. Numerical Biblical decoding by Isaac Newton estimates the year to be 2060, but the Bible also states that the time could be cut short for the sake of the elect, so the exact year is not certain. "The Elect" refers to the first born over all creation, the soul of Christ (through which all human souls are linked to God).

RCMP and Canadian Army Intelligence have known about my identity since 2014 when I brought them messages from God about a possible nuclear first strike, so that the nations could be put on alert. I also passed some other messages, one of which is the fact that God is angry at mankind. God told me to let the leaders of the world know that they do not have as much power as they think they have.

Human society has lapsed into hedonism, greed, and violence throughout history, laced with atheism, idol worship, and perverted Satanic cult activity. Man's savage inhumanity towards man is not the reason for the End Times coming in this century, however. The fate of all human souls is to receive either reward or punishment for eternity on the Day of Judgment, as promised in Scripture. The Last Day must happen at the time of my next death, because my soul has reached its limit for physical existence. After my current incarnation is over, God has assigned to me one final task, which is to be the Judge of all human souls. Then I will lock the Gates of Heaven and Hell forever, so I will be the last soul to see the glorious Heaven that awaits those who are pure enough to gain entry.

Listen, I tell you a mystery: We will not all sleep, but we will all be changed - in a flash, in the twinkling of an eye, at the last trumpet. For the trumpet will sound, the dead will be raised imperishable, and we will be changed. For the perishable must clothe itself with the imperishable, and the mortal with immortality. When the perishable has been clothed with the imperishable, and the mortal with immortality, then the saying that is written will come true: "Death has been swallowed up in victory."

The Creation of Existence

The Creator knows our thoughts, so people tend to go into denial – some consider the very idea of an overseer, a powerful God knowing your thoughts as an invasion of privacy. We could not walk or talk or move our limbs without God's participation, however. The Creator gave us the gift of life, yet people will take it for granted as we happily or unhappily take part in existence and observe ourselves within the world we have been given.

This description of the Creation of the material Universe was observed through the ancient technique of soul travelling. I achieved this through my many years of Tai Chi training, Yoga, fasting, and meditation. This is "The Big Bang".

Various scriptures give clues to scientific and philisophical mysteries that have been the subject of debate for centuries, as well as the cause of division in society when ancient writings lead to misinterpretation. The religious people who cling to traditions from the past refuse to consider updates from God that come in various times and places to match the ability of civilizations to understand the new instructions and the knowledge provided. Judaism stopped advancing at the Old Testament, so they will not accept any teachings of Jesus or Muhammad. Christians express hatred of Islam vehemently, which is contrary to the spirit of love expressed by the words of Jesus, so they have constructed a medieval wall against any new words from God, as they worship the man made Catholic false gods of the Fourth Century. The Christians have become the new Jews, for their churches have already rejected my return and they will not see Heaven.

The term Elohim is plural, and refers to the two souls who were present at Creation - the one God and one mediator mentioned in the Bible. This fact is expressed in Colossians 1:15 *"The son is the image of the invisible God, the firstborn over all creation. For in him all things were created, things in Heaven and on earth, visible or invisible, whether thrones or dominions or rulers or authorities. All things were created through him and for him. He is before all things, and in him all things hold together."* This proves that I was the first soul created by God before the universe came into being.

In Physics, matter is a wave of vibrating frequencies that needs a mediating force that will enable the wave to collapse into particle form. In Philosophy, we wonder what is the reason for existence, and the phrase "all things were created for him and through him" reveals that the Christ Consciousness is the mediating factor that answers both those questions. Material life provides content for the consciousness which would not be available in purely spiritual existence. All life forms are connected to God through the Christ Consciousness, and there are many forms of life throughout the vast universe.

In the beginning of the plan for a physical universe in which physical beings could share the joy of existence God put together the countless codes, formulas, programs, and streams of energy that would bring about an environment suitable for physical life forms.

The Supreme Being is the omnipresent energy who always was and always will be. In His purity and benevolence, the almighty One had existed alone for eons in contentment. God is creative beyond what we can imagine.

The Creator wanted to share the joy of existence and have another soul around so there could be interaction and conversation. Being omnipresent He felt no sense of borders for He was already in existence everywhere. He is all-powerful so He could not create an equal entity; the first soul created would have to be a lesser being, one able to travel and to arrive at set points to experience suffering and to enjoy the various adventures available in the state of aware existence. God said `Let there be light ` then there was light, and God saw that the light was good. He called the light Yeshua (Jesus Christ): the messiah would do His work and carry the Word. God never takes physical form, but the light could be both a wave and particle to walk the material plane for Him. Angelic souls were brought into existence, but they lacked depth of character from never experiencing suffering. A third of the angels split away with Lucifer the proud Archangel who rebelled against God, the angels loyal to God were given set tasks and functions. Angels are non-material beings. Sometimes higher-ranking Archangels Michael and Gabriel can be sent to appear on earth temporarily in material form. The messiah's experiences would consist of the struggle among humans between good and evil. Add to Heaven the music of passion...Classical masterpieces of Mozart and the Blues - all types of music expressing woe and difficult moments in life in artistic form. All events, all moments, all intentions of independent souls are recorded forever in God's consciousness.

The Universe, the material plane, came into existence by God's will and was set into motion by a powerful blast of sound that sent vibrations out at many frequencies. These signals would settle as matter interacting with life forms through the universal Buddha Christ consciousness – the mediator of fields. No one has been to Heaven or Hell yet; these are still under construction and will be ready when they are needed – all souls reincarnate over and over until Judgment Day. God states that He made life from the raw material of love. The Creator would continue to create because matter wears out and decays; the vibration would fade eventually as He designed the Universe so that better futures would evolve. Existence tumbled into the void. The loop was at the end of the cosmos; the last event; the withering separation of light into weak & strong nuclear energies. Gravity, the powerful sister, stood helplessly by. The vacuum stole its grasp on the disappearing particles. Her yielding attractive brother, the electromagnetic host of awareness gently listened to the strings and contemplated the music of the dying universe to its last vibrating strand. Gravity became a notion - a call for assistance, and then was joined by the timid host to turn the oscillating loop around. They were the Yin-Yang, substantial and insubstantial seeking an inhabited pinpoint to direct, one of six types of quark that could cause light to shine as a plume of electrons to feed the build-up of energy created by the movement between the two realms of being and non-being where dimensions meet.

The absolute imperative, the Creator made some changes, allowing chaos and attraction to touch. By His will and His Word, the explosion of existence roared; vibrations sprang forward on a data-filled river of time. This Universe, this splendidly seeded field would grow once more, thrive, then decay as the once enthusiastic energy would inevitably become tired like all living things; its consciousness would one day long for dissipation, not appreciating its creation nor expecting rebirth. The cycle of the living Universe with its crops of civilizations would repeat endlessly however because that which has been created will never be un-created, adjustments are made, and the design will evolve, striving to get closer to impossible perfection. God can step in and reboot the system at any point; He is omnipotent, omnipresent, self-aware, and exists outside of relativity, space, and time without visual form since He is always everywhere maintaining His creations throughout the vast Universe.

The practitioner of soul travelling, or "guru" must not eat, sleep, or drink water for several days in order to roll out of the physical body and to travel in space and time. Those skilled in Spiritual Yoga, known as Kundalini, can perform soul travelling safely. If God has something important to say to you, He will inform you during meditation. The technique of being still in the lotus or prone positions will decelerate bodily functions so you can take your mind away from the material world. The creative energy of the soul is compared to a coiled-up snake that rises up through the 'Chakras', which are seven basic energy centers from the base of the spine to the crown. The goal is to awaken these centers one at a time in a procedure that will prevent physical damage from the energy. You will be unleashing the full power of your life force.

In Sanskrit, the word 'chakra' means 'disk' or 'wheel' and refers to the energy centers in your body. Each disk of spinning energy corresponds to certain nerve bundles and major organs. Spiritual healers use a twelve-chakra system to include energy points outside of the body. There is a chakra below that is rooted into the earth and there are four spiritual energy centers above the head. At the base of the spine is the Root Chakra, then the Sacral Chakra just below navel level, then the Solar Plexus, Heart, Throat, Third Eye, and Crown Chakras.

Blessed are the poor in spirit, for theirs is the kingdom of heaven. Blessed are those who mourn, for they shall be comforted. Blessed are the meek, for they shall inherit the earth. Blessed are those who hunger and thirst for righteousness, for they shall be satisfied. Blessed are the merciful, for they shall receive mercy. Blessed are the pure in heart, for they shall know God. Blessed are the peacemakers, for they shall be called the children of God. Blessed are those who hunger and thirst for righteousness' sake, for theirs is the kingdom of heaven.

When you pray, you must not be like the hypocrites who love to stand and pray in the churches s and at the street corners, that they may be seen by others. Truly, I say to you, they have received their reward. But when you pray, go into your room and shut the door and pray to your Father who is in secret. And your Father who sees in secret will reward you. And when you pray, do not chant or heap up empty phrases as the pagans do, for they think that they will be heard for their many words. Do not be like them, for your Father knows what you need before you ask him.

I do not need to receive glory from mankind - I expect obedience. The Father who sent me, He has testified of me. You have not seen His form at any time, nor heard His voice. You search the Scriptures that testify about me, thinking that in the pages you will find everlasting life, yet you are most unwilling to come to me so that you may have life. I know you, and I know you do not have love for God in your hearts. I have come in my Father's name and you do not receive me, but others come in their own names, yet you receive them. How can you say you are believers in God when you glorify one another? You do not seek the glory that is the one and only God. You glorify the false prophets and greedy priests. Those who love the things of this world are the enemies of God.

It is human nature to be stubbornly proud rather than curious and humble. The puzzle of life is complex, so it is necessary to understand the purpose of life and to rise above the negative conditioning to which all people are exposed. Apathy cannot bring satisfaction, for not caring will bring no accomplishments. Getting something done successfully is a satisfying event. Fulfilling our spiritual responsibilities has a calming effect, while catering to our material responsibilities brings anxiety and stress. The happiness of your soul can be stolen from you, just as thieves can take away your money and property. There are people who mislead others into false ideas by telling them what they want to hear instead of the truth.

The nations have been fighting with each other for ages, so we should strive for a golden age of secure peace where all people can enjoy the time remaining until Judgment Day. The faithful have no fear of the inevitable end of mankind's physical existence, since it will mean entrance into the eternal bliss of Heaven and freedom from the drudgery of life. Most of the world's population are disbelievers who will scoff at any such notion of life after death, so they will find the truth after they are sent to be punished forever in Hell. The atheists are very bad gamblers, for their pride has caused them to bet everything on an empty pot. Those who have misled others into false religions to enrich themselves financially are just as foolish, thinking that God does not know their intentions.

Isaiah 13:9 "Behold, the day of the Lord comes, cruel, with wrath and fierce anger, to make the land a desolation and to destroy its sinners from it. For the stars of the heavens and their constellations will not give their light; the sun will be dark at its rising, and the moon will not shed its light. I will punish the world for its evil, and the wicked for their iniquity; I will put an end to the pomp of the arrogant, and lay low the pompous pride of the ruthless."

The Underworld and Paradise

Many people live in denial; they do not want to think about death or the afterlife most people do not believe in the afterlife, only oblivion. We are not about to get off the hook that easily – there will be life after death no matter what you believe. Mankind has received many warnings over the centuries through Scriptures in the Old Testament, the New Testament, the Qur'an, and the Dead Sea Scrolls. There will be Judgment Day and the afterlife. It is the responsibility of everyone to study the topics of Heaven and Hell because all souls will be included. A soul does not get an automatic gift of Paradise just for being alive.

On the Last Day, those who meet the requirements for Heaven will sense a "Heavenly body" beneath them. This body can be changed at will for visual beauty to please yourself and others who are pure will be able see and hear you. Streams of pleasure will pour into millions of areas in this new body, which will be yours forever. You can relive any moments from past lifetimes to enjoy over and over – not just one memory at a time but many events simultaneously. That is one of the reasons for reincarnating many times. One life would does not contain enough events to enjoy for eternity; existence would be boring if we had only one life to remember. More importantly, the reincarnation process enables the sculpting of the soul in the material state to become worthy of sharing Heaven in the presence of God, Christ, and the pure souls who will exist with you for eternity. It is unthinkable to miss out on the one chance for Paradise, yet people consider Heaven to be a superstition invented for deceitful purposes.

We are not part of some "single universal consciousness" of one huge soul as some public speakers claim. David Icke is totally wrong telling people such a major falsehood, and he has never had any background to qualify him as an expert in such matters; he should stick to politics instead of spiritual matters. Icke started his career saying he was the son of God, but then he retracted the statement after being ridiculed during interviews. David Icke was a football commentator before he went on to sensationalist speaking tours to expose the Illuminati, after noticing the success of underground reporters such as Alex Jones.

The eternal state of punishment is known variously as "Hell", "Hades", "the Underworld", or "the Lake of Fire" so this is a place to avoid at all costs. It will cost you only your sins to come to God – it will cost you your soul if you do not obey the Lord who created you and His servant the prophet Jesus Christ, who is Buddha and Muhammad.

Hell will be tailor-made to a person's worst fears. It will be a wretched existence for the sinners and the disbelievers. Not all those who cry out "Lord, Lord" will enter the Kingdom of Heaven. The function of Satan the devil is to torment the souls of the wicked for all eternity. Those who are cast into Hades will be sorry they ever got born. The Underworld environment will be a sense of horror, pain, humiliation, and loneliness without the presence of God or His son Jesus Christ.

In Hell there will be no parole system, no escape, no hope for tomorrow, for each day will be a repeat of the previous day's anguish. Instead of being connected, those souls in Hell will be isolated forever in solitary despair. There will a great weeping and the gnashing of teeth.

Life is ultimately a test, so it is important to study whenever possible to ensure that you pass. Human nature has led to ignorance, irresponsibility, egotism, and bitterness. Those souls who can rise above the plastic personalities who surround us with their endless lies can find satisfaction. When you have the sword of truth in your hand and God on your side then you can win the battles and claim victory in your spiritual strength.

Dwelling on the past and the obsession with trivial matters is self-destructive. The human ego is easily bruised, so people will lash out defensively when confronted with the truth. There is an ongoing debate about extraterrestrials, the day of the Sabbath, or the shape of the earth when there are heavier priorities to face. What will you do if the world ends tomorrow, and you find yourself trapped in Hell forever? At that point it will not make any difference whether the planet is spherical, flat, or a cube. It will not matter if you rested on Saturday or Sunday if you failed to obey the Commandments of God by spreading messages of hate against your enemies or ignoring God throughout your life. Once you fail Judgment your soul will be condemned forever. Those who are sent to the Underworld will remain there in fear and pain for eternity.

The reason that souls reincarnate many times is to store up enough experiences and memories to last for eternity, which is an unimaginably long time. The soul would become bored re-living only one lifetime's worth of events, so God has provided for eternal entertainment for the pure and righteous people who have obeyed God's Commandments. It is not necessary to convert to Christianity to heed the communication from God through one of my reincarnations as a prophet. In other lifetimes my contribution to upgrading society was done through music and science. Leonardo and Mozart are prime examples, so all philosophies can trust the words that God has conveyed to mankind. Consider these verses when contemplating your destiny:

2 Corinthians 5:10 "We must all appear before the Judgment seat of Christ, so that each of us may receive what is due to us for the things we have done while in the body, whether good or bad."

Revelation 20:15 "And whosoever was not found written into the book of life was cast into the Lake of Fire."

Hopefully, my instructions will save many people from eternal damnation. A relatively small number of souls will care about themselves enough to take heed in order to avoid the wrath of an angry God at crunch time. The Last Day will not be a day of forgiveness, but a day of vengeance on the evildoers and disbelievers. No one can escape divine justice. You can be confident that those who have victimized you or robbed you will face punishment. Those who think they can get away with anything are only fooling themselves.

There are more than 40,000 cults professing to be Christians, but there can only be one truth; there cannot be 40,000 true doctrines. Most sects have a core belief that Jesus is God, one hundred percent God and one hundred percent human. That make no sense, since two hundred percent does not exist in mathematics, and Jesus Christ is not God. The notion that God took human form on one occasion is pure superstition. Unfortunately, humans are riddled with the desire to have a human god to wave like a flag. The religious leaders speak of the son of God, then they contradict themselves and say that God lowered Himself to have a lifetime as a human being that would allow men to crucify Him and cause Him pain. No one can cause God pain. God created the Christ Consciousness as the first of His acts. In Scripture we see Christ praying to God in the Garden of Gethsemane and on Mount Olivet. Why would God pray to Himself and talk about Himself in the third person? "This is my son, in whom I am well pleased," says the Bible. Jesus never said he was God anywhere in the Scriptures. If you were God, you would certainly be aware of that fact.

God is superior to Jesus Christ, for the Supreme Being is the fountain of all things. God created an only begotten son before the material plane. Through the son He made both the ages and the universe. God made Christ not in semblance but in truth. He made him subsist at His own will as the image of the invisible God – not a divided portion of the Father or a lamp divided into two. Christ was created at the will of God, who gave substance to His glories together with Him. The Father did not deprive Himself of anything He has already in Himself. Because Buddha and Christ are the same soul, all people must treat both names with the same respect.

It is incorrect to say anyone is perfect. Perfection is a poetic term, not scientific. All things must have an element of entropy in order to have a reason to exist. There is no real perfection. God admitted He was sorry He ever created humans, so that was one mistake. Noah and a small group survived the flood, but the rest of mankind was destroyed for being evil. God leaves room to improve and grow, and room to decline and shrink. That is the result of Free Will. Those people who do criminal deeds against others allow the good people to draw a line in the sand between right and wrong, thus strengthening their characters. God has promised not to destroy mankind using a flood ever again; the final destruction will come by fire. That will be Judgment Day, the Last Day of material existence for those on earth. Life will continue throughout the universe, but mankind is intimately attached to the destiny of the Christ Consciousness, so all humans will be judged at the same time. This is due to the limitations of material existence. All souls will continue to be conscious forever. The task of each person is to purify their souls so that they will qualify for Heaven. The purpose of life is to attain eternal Paradise.

Buddhism is usually ignored by those involved in the arguments between Christians, Jews, and Muslims, so they seldom take the time to denounce Buddha, but they condemn Yoga and meditation as evil mystical practices due to their partisan lack of wisdom and distaste for spiritual exploration. The Theology of Islam recognizes the importance of historical Scripture prophets Moses, Jesus, and Muhammad. Judaic belief stops at the Torah, so no further prophets are given credence. Two-thirds of Israel's people are not religious, while the religious Jews do not believe in eternal Hell, and they scorn the name of Jesus and do not recognize any messiah. For some Jews, the name Jesus Christ is associated with pogroms and Crusades, charges of genocide, and centuries of Christian anti-Semitism.

These phrases from the Qur'an give rules to Muslims about self-defensive warlike activities against disbelievers who have attacked or evicted those who believe in God and His messenger. [17:33] "You shall not kill any person - for God has made life sacred - except in the course of justice. If one is killed unjustly, then we give his heir authority to enforce justice. Thus, he shall not exceed the limits in avenging the murder; he will be helped. You may fight in the cause of God against those who attack you, but do not aggress. God does not love the aggressors."

[2:191] "You may kill those who wage war against you, and you may evict them whence they evicted you. Oppression is worse than murder. Do not fight them at the Sacred Masjid, (Great Mosque at Mecca) unless they attack you therein. If they attack you, you may kill them. This is the just retribution for those disbelievers. If they refrain, then God is Forgiver, most merciful. You may also fight them to eliminate oppression, and to worship God freely. If they refrain, you shall not aggress; aggression is permitted only against the aggressors."

[8:12-13] Recall that your Lord inspired the angels: "I am with you; so support those who believed. I will throw terror into the hearts of those who disbelieved. You may strike them above the necks, and you may strike even every finger." This is what they have justly incurred by fighting God and His messenger. For those who fight against God and His messenger, God's retribution is severe.

Important Scriptures

All people must heed the words of God and stop insisting you can save yourselves in eternity. Humans have no control over the reincarnation process, and no control over the ultimate destinations of your souls. Purity is done from within through open mindedness and benevolent thoughts. God knows everybody's intentions so there is nowhere you can hide.

I will list some wise sayings from accepted Biblical Scripture (communication from God through the prophet or disciple as transcribed and translated). The verses contain either universal truths, prophecies, or rules for living properly. The search for truth must include all knowledge from historical sources. These sayings are divine truths rather than inventions of mankind and they will help you attain Enlightenment. God has given knowledge to all cultures at some time.

Matthew 7:1 "Judge not or you will be judged."

This verse speaks about seeing a speck in someone's eye, but you do not see the log in your own eye. What a person measures out will come back to them, and their criticism of others is done to hide their own faults. Many people are automatically confrontational, determined to criticize everyone except themselves. It is human nature to become egotistical and intolerant of others. Those who belittle other people do it to reinforce their own egos.

"Then the Lord saw that the wickedness of man was great on the earth, and that every intent of the thoughts of his heart was only evil continually."

In the Book of Genesis, God becomes angry at mankind and sends a flood to wipe out all people except for Noah and a group of others who built an ark and escaped the first destruction. This is the End Times and God is angry again. The next destruction will be by fire, then Judgment Day. The Bible says that the End Times countdown would begin when mankind got the ability to wipe himself out, after the state of Israel was established. There were enough atom bombs in 1950 to destroy all life, so this situation triggered my birth in 1951 as the Final Messiah. The reference in Scripture is that I am the Alpha and the Omega, the first and last of God's messengers and prophets. The End Times coming in this generation is not because of mankind's failure and indifference to God, the real reason is that my soul has reached its limit for physical reincarnation, so it is time to go home. God spoke to me in March of 2013 for several days and confirmed that I have lived many reincarnations. The soul has an exhaustion point, and God has promised throughout Scripture that all human souls must attend Judgment Day. I will be the First Judge and I may turn away anyone. The souls that God wishes to address will hear his voice at that time. God will upload the information into my consciousness regarding a person's good works, sins, and intentions so my Judgment and His Judgment will likely agree. The Judgment will happen almost simultaneously in Quantum Entanglement, for it is always described as one day. I will be the last soul to see Heaven after I lock the Gates of Hell and Heaven forever. I will then ascend to the throne which has been promised to me.

Matthew 10:33 "Whoever denies me as the messiah on this earth, I will likewise deny before my Heavenly Father on the Day of Judgment."

John 14:6 "Jesus answered them, saying 'I am the Way, the Truth, and the Life; no one comes to the Father but through me."

Qur'an 2:62 "Those who believe in Allah and do righteous things will have their reward with the Lord. There will be no fear concerning them, nor will they grieve."

Proverbs 1:7 "The fear of the Lord is the beginning of knowledge. Fools despise wisdom and instruction. The way of the fool is right in his own eyes, but a wise man listens to advice."

Throughout history God has sent a reminder to every society that has become corrupt, warning them and inviting them to follow the true path. Even still, people persisted in their wickedness and perished after having fulfilled the time allotted to them. The Last Day will be the final calamity to fall upon the world. Those who think that the Qur'an speaks only to a certain group are seriously mistaken – the words given to me when I lived as Muhammad are there to correct the idol worship brought about by the corruption of Christianity into many pagan cults of idol worshipper who long for a human god they can ridicule and dominate. They want a screaming victim to murder so men can feel power over God. Most of the sects of Christianity teach that Jesus and God are the same soul when that is clearly not the truth. God created Jesus Christ before the material universe.

1 Timothy 2:5 "For there is One God and one mediator between God and mankind, the man Christ Jesus."

Colossians 1:15 "The son is the image of the invisible God. Christ is the firstborn over all creation…in him all things were created – things in Heaven and on earth, visible and invisible. He is above all things, whether thrones or dominions or rulers or authorities. All things were created through him and FOR him. He is before all things, and in him all things hold together."

Proverbs 8:22 "The Lord created me at the beginning of His work, the first of His acts of long ago. Ages ago I was set up, at the first…before the beginning of the earth. When there were no depths, I was brought forth – when there were no springs abounding with water. Before the mountains had been shaped, before the hills I was brought forth. When He had not yet made earth or fields or the world's first bits of soil. When He established the heavens, I was there; when He drew a circle on the face of the deep and made firm the skies above, when He established the fountains of the deep and assigned to the sea its limits so the water might not transgress His commands, and when He marked out the foundations of the earth, I was there beside Him like a master worker. I was His daily delight, rejoicing before Him always."

There is no trinity of three equal gods in the Bible or the Qur'an. In the days of Constantine, the church elders burned the writings of the wise man Arius concerning the rebirth of the soul. At the Council of Trent in 325 A.D. they voted in the notion of three god persons who were the same person. This was an effort to satisfy the public who were used to multiple pagan gods. The trinity doctrine is acknowledged by making 'the Sign of the Cross' while calling on the three unclean spirits – the false gods of Rome. That is the Mark of the Beast that is the hidden sin that will condemn all those who believe in the trinity gods made by man.

Revelation 16:3 "And then I saw three unclean spirits coming like frogs from the mouth of the Beast and from the mouth of the false prophet."

The Scriptures always list belief in God as the First Commandment. A person who does not believe in One God is wasting their time taking part in religious activities. Because this is the End Times, we must beware of the prophecies about a world dictatorship taking away all human rights, so spirituality should involve declaring freedom from oppression. All wars have a religious element to them although killing is against God's Commandments. Murder is even more vile when the participants believe that people have only one life to live.

God has said, "Purity of intention runs the show." I will explain how this communication with the Creator came to me in March 2013 after fasting and meditation.

I began training in various martial arts when I was a teenager, starting with Judo and Karate. Later in life I studied Hapkido, Tae Kwon Do, and Wu Style Tai Chi Ch'uan. This prepared me for spiritual enlightenment through disciplines of self-control, modesty, and respect as well as increasing health and self-defence. I got interested in the Chinese art of Tai Chi because it was known as a fountain of youth to practitioners – they tend to live into extreme old age without getting arthritis or heart problems. Like Yoga, Tai Chi stresses the importance of the energy meridians and the chakras. I learned to control my intake of food, since fasting is not part of everyday Western society.

In 2013 I found myself spontaneously fasting and sitting still for several days without a desire for sleep, medicine, food, or water. I switched between the prone and lotus positions at intervals to keep from getting cramps. Then my soul left my body and began to travel. I did not know where I was going, but I could see that I was going through a tunnel and making turns here and there until I came to a room where the walls were an orange color. On one wall was a long geometric formula that was too complex to memorize.

What had happened was part of séance, a project by a gathering of Zen scientists known as The Group of Forty. They had summoned my soul to be the guiding eyes for a small treaded robot camera that was going through a pyramid, ostensibly in Egypt, although I never found out which of the pyramids they were exploring or how they knew the formula for anti-gravity would be there. It had something to do with reincarnation, so I must have been there using the long-lost antigravity technology to build the pyramids.

I felt myself leaving that place, but instead of returning to my body, my soul got hung up in a static state of greyness, with hours of a visual image of a closeup face of a dying man hanging on a cross. This felt like a mysterious test of patience; I was just frozen there for about sixteen hours, then darkness. Out of the darkness came a voice that called out a name I had never heard before:

"Yeshua!"

The tone of the voice was authoritative, so I guessed correctly this was the time to receive my orders. I thought I would lighten the mood a bit, so I replied with a joke after hearing "Yeshua".

"Gesundheit" I said, to lighten the atmosphere with a quip. God spoke back right away:

"Listen and do not speak. Have no fear, you are not dead. I have brought you here for a special reason. Do you know that mankind is awfully egotistical thinking they are the only intelligent life forms in the Universe? In fact, there are over ten thousand more advanced civilizations in the Milky Way Galaxy alone."

At that point God revealed that Earth was not the original planet were humans were first positioned. He had transported mankind to this planet from a different galaxy as a suitable place for development. It appears that we are the aliens. God then continued His introduction.

"And do you know that mankind is very ignorant and irresponsible believing that there was no Creator involved in all of this? I am that Creator and I have brought you into existence for the last time as the third and final Full scripture messiah. You will prepare humanity for the Ascension and Judgment Day. After this reincarnation, your services will be required one more time - that is to be the First Judge of human souls on the Day of Judgment. You will be the last soul to see Heaven, where you will take the throne that I have promised you. Then you will lock the gates of Heaven and Hell forever. Of course, you know about being Jesus in a past life, and now it is time for Christianity and Islam to unite, because Jesus and Muhammad were the same man. I do not want to give you a big head, but you were also the person who lived the lives of Buddha, Leonardo da Vinci, and Mozart. You are the first and last – you were all the messiahs. I did not give you any Scripture when you were Buddha; I let you figure out everything for yourself using your own common sense. Buddha lived at a place and time when most people around him were atheists, so Buddhism became a secular philosophy of understanding how to cope with the suffering of life by forsaking the attachment for worldly things."

"Now you will bring my Final Covenant to the human race. I am making you responsible for the souls of every person on earth, and I am giving you authority over all Scripture. You must bring the people back to God and put an end to war. This will be your most important life, your greatest mission of all – the task of bringing the faithful to Heaven. Present yourself as Jesus Christ since in that incarnation you did not get to live a full lifespan and the teachings of Jesus led the way. The reason for the End coming at this time has something to do with you is that after so many lifetimes your soul has become exhausted. I promise this will be your last reincarnation, then you will finally rejoin me in Heaven. I want to apologize for your current incarnation for you have gone through much pain, but as an early reward I am going to allow you to live for a short time as three of your most influential incarnations."

Suddenly I began to see visual shapes again. Three ovals appeared in front of me, and within them were images of Jesus, Buddha, and Prophet Muhammad all speaking to small groups of people. I was drawn into all three time zones simultaneously and found myself inside their bodies looking outward and thinking as they thought. This phenomenon lasted about ten minutes, long enough for me to understand how all three philosophies fit together. All three settings were calm areas in lightly wooded fields where I was speaking to a small group in each.

God told me that He was able to bring me into three past lifetimes as the maximum simultaneous existences possible, or else my soul would get the bends.

I had more miraculous experiences in that seven days at the Godhead (God called this place the fifth dimension in a ten-dimensional Universe). The Creator allowed me a sample of the experience of what Heaven will be like in the future. I felt suspended in a Heavenly body for several minutes with rapid pulses of pleasure. God told me that the souls who make it to Heaven will be able to summon up any past happy memories from several lifetimes at once in a simultaneous flood of joy and satisfaction. Pain and hardship will no longer be in their memories, and they will know only happiness.

The dimension of the Heavenly Plane consists of an unknown number of angels, higher-ranking archangels such as Gabriel and Michael, the 24 souls of the Council of Elders, then God Himself.

There is a military air about the system; there will be various ranking layers of reward and punishment after Judgment, when all the souls that have been created will be brought to be Judged and receive their sentence, whether good or bad. That is why I urge people to wake up and learn the requirements for salvation from eternal punishment.

There are many cults in the world who think they have the right to Heaven despite holding beliefs that are false, invented to build a following, or based on superstition or greed. Some notable cults are Scientology, the NAR (New Apostolic Reformation), Christian Evangelism, the Hare Krishna movement, Zionism, Freemasonry, Satanism, Seventh Day Adventists, the Church of England, Mormonism, and the pagan cult of Mary, which consists of Roman Catholicism and Eastern Orthodox churches.

Cults use indoctrination to attract and hold members in their grip. The brainwashing sessions often start with music to hypnotize the audience into a state of readiness and acceptance. Then the preacher or priest will make all sorts of claims that they have the exclusive knowledge and the understanding of God's will. Christian televangelists will pretend to heal people or put on an act that they are speaking in tongues in their stage shows. Most of the commercial preachers will tell people that they are channelling God's thoughts. Some cult leaders like Vissarion in Russia and A.J. Miller in Australia pretend to be Jesus Christ without offering a shred of evidence, yet they have millions of devout followers. Pastor Apollo Quiboloy in the Philippines also claims to be Jesus, which gives him a luxurious lifestyle complete with private jets and mansions in a country where people make less than two dollars a day. He will still take their money. People will listen to anything except the truth.

There is a long list of liars who claim they speak to God: Jimmy Swaggart, Joyce Meyer, Benny Hinn, Mark Taylor, Kim Clement, Joel Osteen, Kenneth Copeland, Jim Bakker, and many more. They all take in millions of dollars every year in donations from gullible followers.

The commercial evangelists live in fine mansions; they own private jets and yachts, but they always ask for more money. Although their hypocrisy is obvious, their followers keep sending money.

The many religions of the world have splintered into countless belief systems, so there is no consensus on a correct doctrine. There can be only one truth, not many. Monotheism is that truth. As soon as an institution decides to spread out God's glory to other beings and physical men, they are on a path that will lead their followers away into the abyss of ignorance, and ultimately to eternal damnation in Hell.

Governments and leaders like to use God's name to justify their policies, which include killing real or imagined enemies, deceiving the public with false news, and allowing corporations to dictate laws. The politicians swear an oath to work on behalf of the people, then they promptly break their oaths by working for special interest groups instead. Elected leaders swear to tell the truth and then proceed to uphold a constant string of lies to deceive the voters. God has promised to send liars into the Lake of Fire, so those who tell lies do not believe in God.

Many disbelievers will never change, no matter how much evidence they are shown to the contrary. No one can prove that all things came from nothing, yet they still insist that is the case. If there was a wandering sub-atomic particle that inflated into the universe, it must have come from somewhere. The laws of mathematics did not just fall together by accident, there are codes, laws, programs, and the phenomenon of consciousness to explain. There has been a concerted effort by certain elite societies to promote atheism over the past several centuries. The removal of God from people's thoughts set the stage for trendy materialistic values to take over from spiritual and moral values of the past.

Spiritual responsibility goes hand in hand with social responsibility. No one needs to become a martyr for religious beliefs or submit to persecution by disbelievers. People have suffered whenever populations have surrendered to tyrants, so it becomes necessary to defend oneself with strong ideas and legal actions. If the rulers of nations could be made to learn the truth, some would change their ways. They would not want divine justice to be waiting for them when they die. Some of the enemies of righteousness might defect and reveal the truth.

Religious politicians are extremely dangerous since they wish to destroy anyone who does not agree with them. The New World Order uses the fascist blueprint to subjugate nations. Adolf Hitler believed he was on a mission from God, so he felt justified in murdering others. The popes of history have started wars of Crusade and carried on ruthless Inquisitions where millions were tortured and murdered for any transgression that seemed to be against the church's rigid doctrines.

Even though we live in the Twenty-First Century, the pope still wants total control over all countries and people. The popes have been historically aggressive because they are evil. Benito Mussolini made the Vatican a nation-state in 1932, so they have diplomatic immunity. Organized crime launders its money through Vatican banks, and the church is involved in massive drug smuggling operations and child sex slavery rings around the world. They use a private intelligence network, known as the Jesuit Army of Loyola, to carry out their plots. All wars since the French Revolution were engineered by the Jesuits.

The Plot Against Mankind

Ephesians 6:12 "For we wrestle not against flesh and blood, but against principalities, against powers, against the rulers of the darkness of this world, against spiritual wickedness in high places."

Although the Bible used today has many contradictions after sixteen centuries of Vatican editing, it has astonishing prophecies that tell about the coming of the dictatorial forces that we see running most of the world in these times. The situation is that a fascist cabal of unelected rich people are trying to gain power above sovereign nations by declaring fictitious world emergencies in matters of health and the environment so that they can remove all personal rights. Those who are in police and military positions would be wise to resist before they are deemed redundant and replaced by United Nations personnel.

A democracy cannot exist as a permanent form of government, it can only exist until the politicians learn that they can vote themselves money from the public treasury. From then on, the majority always votes for the candidates promising the most benefits for their causes, with the result that a democracy always collapses over loose fiscal policy, always followed by a dictatorship. The average age of the world's greatest civilizations has been two hundred years. These nations have progressed through a sequence where people go from bondage to spiritual faith, from spiritual faith to great courage; from courage to liberty; from liberty to abundance, from abundance to selfishness, from selfishness to apathy, from apathy to dependence, and then from dependence back into bondage. The way things are going, mankind is about to be trampled by the globalists.

Spirituality should not be used to hide from the world's political problems. Citizens can hide for a short time from government oppression, so it is fair to resist the encroachment of personal freedoms. The power brokers do not want people to assemble, for it could lead to resistance. They do not want their lies to be exposed so they take away freedom of speech and freedom of the press. Small businesses have been closed or taxed out of existence.

People should be allowed to live full lives and to grow into old age. Society should respect the elderly, for much wisdom is needed to help the young. Decadence seldom leads to old age, and never to wisdom. Popular culture is shallow but full of glitter to impress the eye. Idols in costumes strive to implant envy so that others will desire admiration from faceless and nameless strangers for no other reason than to foster for themselves a fantasy of illusory glory.

All the nations of the world are under physical and psychological attack, and all people are targets of the New World Order fanatics who worship Satan. The financial oligarchs are a monolithic cult of psychopaths who have committed genocide for centuries in their desire to depopulate the earth. They have set up police states where they can take people from their homes and place them in detention camps where they will be inoculated with poisonous vaccines using the excuse of protecting the public from fictitious virus strains. All people must resist.

The wealthy elites who control the world's resources believe in destruction and death. They are against life, happiness, and equality. Evil begets evil, so their family bloodlines carry on the wicked policies and practices of previous villains. Secret societies partake in blood rituals complete with child sacrifice, Adrenochrome harvesting, blood drinking, and cannibalism. The truth is coming to light about the decadent corruption of the criminals who rule the nations. They concoct fake epidemics to cause widespread fear with an endless barrage of propaganda designed to destroy society as they anticipate profits from the toxic potions and equipment related to the business of medical tyranny. The newly equipped and well-padded police forces are there to enforce the isolation of people, the occult symbolism of masking people, and the closing of small businesses for no good reason.

"Social Distancing" is a torture technique invented by the CIA. There is no medical evidence saying that isolating people stops illness; it is more liable to cause depression, anxiety, and thoughts of suicide.

The COVID mania is fuelled by corporate media who say whatever is put in front of them. It is better not to listen to the mainstream news since it is part of the psychological attack on the population. The major media outlets are owned by the same cabal of elitists who belong to secret societies. The best place for a television set is in the garbage dumpster. The Orwellian fear messages will damage the recipients of their programming. The World Economic Forum wants people to believe they are helplessly under attack from mutating viruses. There is no scientific basis for this claim.

Viruses are created from within your cells; they do not come from outside the body. They arise as a result of systemic toxicity, not because the body has been invaded by an external threat. Part of immune response is to create viruses to clean up poisons. Viruses dissolve toxic matter when body tissue is too toxic for living bacteria or microbes to feed upon without being poisoned to death. Without viruses, the human body could not achieve homeostasis and sustain itself in the face of systemic toxicity. Viruses are specific; they dissolve specific tissues in the body. They do this with the assistance of antibodies. Viruses are discriminatory by nature, made by the body for a specific purpose. They are not indiscriminate killers. Viruses are Exosomes - solvents for toxic cells. The more toxicity you have in your body, the more viral activity you will have. The only vector transmission of a virus is through blood transfusion or vaccines. Viruses cannot infect you by jumping from one body to another.

In addition to aborted human fetus tissue, the vaccine industry relies on DNA from species such as birds, dogs, monkeys, cows, pigs, mice and insects in vaccine manufacturing. Other deadly ingredients are mercury, liquid aluminum, formaldehyde, nickel, and chemicals used as antifreeze for cars. The ingredients are not vegetarian by any means, they are cannibalistic.

The human immune system is more than capable of dealing with illness when the person is healthy and not full of toxins.

Over many centuries the Vatican has planned to engineer its return to total world domination. Their banks launder money for the Mafia and the cardinals and bishops are pedophiles of the worst kind – it is part of their religion that the priests believe they can forgive each other's sins, so they have no remorse over ruining the lives of their many victims. All wars since the French Revolution were put into motion by the Jesuit Army of Loyola, the pope's spy network of provocateurs, planners, and infiltrators. The Rothschild family owns most of the central banks, and becasue they print the money, they control the Vatican, the Zionists, Freemasons, Skull and Bones, the Illuminati, the Federal Reserve Banks, the Knights of Malta, and most politicians. The wealthy elites do not care about poor people at all.

The Canon Law of the Council of Trent is still in effect: "All those who do not bow to the pope are heretics who must be put to death." (Thomas Aquinas) The objective of the Cult of Rome is to enslave mankind under a papal dictatorship run by corporate interests. The institutions are led by pedophiles who have given their souls to the devil in their greed and perversion.

The Vietnam War was started to protect Catholic business interests in industries such as rubber, bauxite, opium, offshore oil, tungsten, timber, and coal. The genocide of Buddhists was the result. Vietnam had been a French colony, so European Catholicism was well entrenched. The policy was to herd people into 'Strategic Hamlets' with military posts on the perimeters. The people in the hamlets would be urged into accepting Catholicism in return for protection. Buddhist were persecuted rather than accepted. Catholicism maintains a dogma that there is no salvation outside of the Catholic church. A dogmatic belief is one which must be believed by the members of the sect. They honestly believe that no one can go to Heaven without the pope's blessing, so the brainwashing is effective. Catholics must believe that the pope cannot make a mistake, and that the communion wafer turns into flesh once blessed by the priest. They also believe that someone named Mary is monitoring mankind's thoughts and that she has divine powers to enforce Heavenly Law and answer prayers. The list of nonsensical doctrines includes the dogma that three god persons are one god person who is not aware of his magical triune nature since they talk about each other and to each other in the third person. Over the centuries the yellow brick road has branched off into many detours.

It is human nature to be stubbornly proud rather than curious and humble. The puzzle of life is complex, so it is necessary to understand the purpose of life and to rise above the negative conditioning to which all people are exposed. Apathy cannot bring satisfaction, for not caring will bring no accomplishments. Getting something done successfully is a satisfying event. Fulfilling our spiritual responsibilities has a calming effect, while catering to our material responsibilities brings anxiety and stress. The happiness of your soul can be stolen from you, just as thieves can take away your money and property. There are people who mislead others into false ideas by telling them what they want to hear instead of the truth.

Vatican City was granted status as a nation-state by Mussolini in 1933. It is time to reverse the policy of Benito Mussolini and shut down all operations of the Catholic system, including its universities, churches, orphanages, and other institutions of indoctrination. The Synagogue of Satan must be exposed for what it is: a power hungry political machine bent on ruling the world; it is not a proper religion, but a cult of evildoers pretending to be righteous citizens. The church is really the Nazi party under another name.

The fraudulent pandemic lie has been used by the elites of the New World Order to commit premeditated murder. It is calculated and cunning in nature, since it began with the Jesuit planners who engineer all the wars on behalf of the Catholic crime syndicate posing as a legitimate religion. Every death soon after the injection of any experimental drug from Pfizer, Johnson and Johnson, Moderna and others must then be suspected as part of the bigger picture of premeditated medically assisted death. The fatal results of these experimental injections must be considered as cases of culpable homicide.

Genocide, war, and murder are nothing new to the Catholic cult: the devotees of Mary have a long history of violence to force their pagan religion onto innocent people through the Crusades, Inquisitions, and global wars designed to thin out populations before their victims could offer strong resistance to the tyranny of the popes. The wizards who call themselves 'holy men' are still devils in dresses who are obsessed with sexual depravity, sadism, and torture. Over 10,000 priests have been arrested in the last few decades for molesting children - the very reason they became priests in the first place. The priesthood is a closed society where everything in life is supplied by the church, so the misfits who are afraid of real work can live in luxury while they stalk children in their ample spare time.

There is no lower creature in society than a Catholic priest. The priesthood is a males-only cult of morally crippled snakes who are profoundly backward in religious thought, yet they insist on promoting the false teachings in which they were indoctrinated since childhood. Priests are greedy parasites who siphon off the donations of honest people for their own purposes. The Catholic church does not give money to the poor: they adorn their cathedrals and dine on the finest food while others starve. Priests learn to bury their consciences in the putrid swill of their incessant lies. The priests spend their lives deceiving others and leading the people into eternal damnation using a corrupt theology based on superstition, fear, myths, and mysticism. They claim to possess magic powers to turn wafers into the flesh of Jesus, and they say they can change water into the blood of Christ. If you blink, you might miss their little miracles.

Priests are predators ready to snatch up their prey in a spider's web of doubletalk. The false doctrines of Catholicism confuse the logical thinker, so many people quit religion forever due to the hypocrisy of the Vatican agents and their brainwashed flocks of dreamy-eyed zombies. Rome has left a legacy of lies that Orthodox churches have retained as their truths - the worship of Mary, the division of God into three minor characters known as the holy trinity, veneration of elected saints, and the transubstantiation of the flesh during the communion ceremony. All of these doctrines are anti-Biblical; there are no sacraments in the Scriptures.

There is no divine being called Mary in the Bible, and no instruction to pray to her. The Bible says there is One God and one mediator, yet today over a billion people have been led to believe that there are three gods under the control of their mother, the imaginary goddess Mary. Idol worship is rampant in Catholicism. The churchgoers cry and kiss statues of Mary in their hysteria over someone who does not exist. Images and icons adorn the churches to offer many beings as divinities worthy of receiving prayers. When a person accepts several more gods, the sky's the limit - more divine beings can be added into the mix at will, since the souls involved have trashed the First and Second Commandments totally by defining God as a triune mystery. The festering sore of the Vatican can be cured by cutting it away with the Sword of Truth.

In my 2013 communication from the Creator, God calls mankind "egotistical, self-centered, ignorant, and irresponsible" so it is up to each person to improve and start thanking God for existence. If you have ignored God, simply say you are sorry and ask for forgiveness. There is no other entity who knows all your thoughts, so it is useless to pray to any other entity. God is disappointed with the society that has developed from mankind's greed. Most people have turned their backs on God totally. The cult of the 'self' has replaced spiritual awareness of universal harmony and peace with your neighbors. When national leaders are atheists, they are not motivated to behave properly. They will lie, cheat, and steal as much as possible.

All people are alive so that they can coexist and help each other to advance. It would be possible to feed the hungry and give shelter to the homeless if the funds were not used up on security services, national interference, and lining the pockets of the wealthy corporate elite. The wealthy are organized as a monolithic cult, and they pass the tradition of occultism and perversion through their children. The people at the top have been indoctrinated to have no consciences; they hate life and continually start wars so that the lower classes can kill all the strong young people who might rebel against them.

All that evil needs to triumph is for good people to do nothing. The Zen Buddhist and Taoist concept of "do nothing" does not refer to social laziness; the term describes the stillness of the mind. Relaxation is a major key to overall fitness. When you can relax the muscles, it is easier to maintain good balance. It is possible to improve control over the body with exercises that work on breathing, balance, relaxation, and concentration. The healthiest diet is vegetarian for various reasons. Those who have a diet based on animal meat die at a younger age; they develop arterial plaque, obesity, cancer, and high blood pressure. It seems natural to have a love for animals, so the moral implications of slaughtering them is repugnant to Buddhists.

Reality is ultimately an illusion where each consciousness takes part in assembling what is to come by interacting with events within the 'dharma' - the order of things as set out by the laws of the universe. There are mathematical laws, physical laws, moral laws, and spiritual laws. To give an example, let's say a subject has abused himself by becoming a crack cocaine addict.

God told me that smoking crack stretches the geometry of the human soul into a state of permanent damage due to the potency and speed of delivery to the nervous system. The high is euphoric because the soul is breaking into a level higher than the material dimension artificially. Users compare crack smoking to having a taste of instant paradise. They are using up potential future rewards, but the effect is tantalizing and addictive. Many users will divert large amounts of money to purchase a steady supply, so they will resort to stealing to get the necessary money. Self-indulgence is morally wrong in the first place, so all the laws get broken in the desire for sensual pleasure immediately. It is morally wrong to deprive others of their property for your own personal pleasure.

The lucrative drug industry has affected modern society adversely, whether those substances are illegal or pharmaceutical. Chemical drugs are different from the naturally occurring organic drugs such as THC, psilocybin mushrooms, or peyote cactus. Opium comes from poppies, but it has strong addictive qualities, and so should be avoided. Opium has a long history of causing misery in countries like China, where American and British distributers got wealthy by supplying the drug to the population. Opium is the base for manufacturing morphine and heroin. There are also many artificial opiates that cause overdose deaths due to higher potency. Marijuana and hashish are derived from the cannabis plant, a type of hemp. The medical benefits of THC are numerous and cannibis is non-addictive.

Most pharmaceutical products are made from petroleum and are therefore toxic. Lipstick, makeup, allergy pills, cold pills, and other over-the-counter products have poisons in them. The suppliers of many types of consumer goods and fast foods are deliberately getting people to ingest toxins all through life.

Here is some text from the John D. Rockefeller -" *We will keep their lives short and keep their minds weak while pretending to do the opposite. We will use our knowledge of science and technology in subtle ways so that they never see what is happening. We will use soft metals, aging accelerators and sedatives in food and water as well as in the air. They will* be covered in poisons wherever they turn. The soft metals will make them lose their minds. We will promise to find a cure from our many funds, and yet we will give them more poison. Chemical poisons will be absorbed through the skin of idiots who believe that certain hygiene and beauty products presented by great actors and musicians, will bring eternal youth to their faces and bodies, and through their thirsty and hungry mouths, we will destroy their minds and systems of internal organs. reproduction. However, their children will be born as disabled and deformed and we will hide this information. The poisons will be hidden in everything around them, in what they drink, eat, breathe, and wear. We must be ingenious in distributing the poisons because they can see far. We will teach them that poisons are good - with funny pictures and musical tones on TV. Those who are looking for them will be helpful. We will enroll them to push our poisons. They will see that our products are used in film and they will get used to them and will never know their true effect.

When they give birth, we will inject poisons into the blood of their children and convince them that we are helping them! We will start earlier, when their minds are young, we will target their children with what children love most - sweet things. When their teeth decay, we will fill them with metals that will kill their minds and steal their future. When their ability to learn has been affected, we have created drugs that will make them sicker and cause them other illnesses, for which we will create even more drugs. We will make them docile and weak before us, by our power. They will grow depressed, slow and obese, and when they come to us for help, we will give them more poison. We will focus our attention on money and material goods so that they never connect with their inner self. We will distract them with fornication, external pleasures, and video games, so that they are never one with the unity of all.

Their minds will belong to us, and they will do as we say. If they refuse, we will find ways to implement technology that alters the mind in their lives. We will use fear as our weapon. We will establish their governments and we will establish opposition within them. We will own both sides.

We will always hide our goal, but we will continue our plan. They will do the work for us, and we will prosper from their toil. Our families will never mix with theirs. Our blood must be pure (because it is). We will make them kill each other when they oppose us. We will keep them separate from unity through dogma and religion. We will control all aspects of their lives and tell them what to think and how. We will guide them kindly and let them believe that they are guiding themselves. We will instigate animosity among them through our factions. When a light shines among them, we will extinguish it by mockery or death, which suits us best. We will make them tear their hearts apart and kill their own children. We will accomplish this using hatred as our ally, anger as our friend. Hatred will completely blind them and they will never see that in their conflicts we will be their leaders. They will be busy killing each other. They will bathe in their own blood and kill their neighbors, as long as we see that they are against us.

We will benefit greatly from this, for they will not see us, for they cannot see us. We will continue to prosper from their wars and their deaths. We will repeat this until our goal is achieved. We will continue to make them live in fear and anger, we will give them images and sounds. We will use all the tools we have to achieve this. The tools will be provided by their work. We will make them hate themselves and their neighbors. We will always hide the divine truth from them, that we are all one. That he must never know! They must never know that color is an illusion, they must always believe that they are not equal.

Drop by drop, drop by drop we will advance our goal. We will take over their lands, resources, and wealth to exercise control over them. We will trick them into accepting laws that will steal the little freedom they have. We will set up a money system that will shut them down forever, keeping them and their children in debt. When we ban them altogether, we will accuse them of murder and present a different story to the world because we will own all the media. We will use the media to control the flow of information and their feelings in our favor. When they revolt against us, we will crush them like insects, because they are less than that. They will be helpless to do anything about it."

The secret societies are all connected in this plot: Freemasons, Zionists, Jesuits, Skull and Bones, the Knights of Malta, the Illuminati, the Federal Reserve banks, the Council on Foreign Relations, the CIA, and the Bilderberg Group. They are called the New World Order. Those who are not part of the solution are part of the problem. It is up to the people to resist oppression.

Groups such as the Rockefeller Foundation, the United Nations, the Bill and Melinda Gates Foundation, the Center for Disease Control, and the World Economic Forum have made extensive plans to depopulate the earth. Eugenics includes acts of Euthanasia, where those deemed to be a burden on society are exterminated. Purges also attack individuals who oppose the policies of the regime and those who may present a potential future threat. Free thinkers, intellectuals, artists, musicians, and scientists are often the targets of totalitarian rulers.

Agenda 21 is a code name for a master plan that originated at the United Nations to change the political and economic systems of the world to one of total collectivism. In order to do that, people must not be allowed to have independence; they must be put into a position where they are dependent on the state for everything. That makes it possible for the state to control them. This means private property will be phased out and people will not be able to have land of their own. They will have to live in high rise apartments that are provided by the state for free as a benefit, luring people into the cities and away from the hinterland.

The people at the top who hold the strings of power do not want anyone living out in the country because those who own land and have a water supply can grow their own food, so that person or family are not dependent on the generosity of the state. Those who own a few acres of land are a threat to the globalist agenda. The wealthy elites do not have to beg the politicians for food or shelter. The New World Order does not want citizens living in the country; they want the big corporations to own and control the farmland. The factory farms are replacing the family farms, with people like Bill Gates buying up all the land so that the oligarchs who manipulate the money supply can also control the food supply.

The elites do not want anyone living outside of big cities. They want the population to be easy to control, herded into ghettos from which they cannot travel, and to be inoculated with deadly toxins that will shorten your life. That is the dirty secret of Agenda 21 – the depopulation of the earth. The number of people in the world is estimated at eight billion, so they aim to reduce this number to less than one billion. That goal can only be reached by increasing their massive campaigns of genocide. Tanzanian president John Magufuli was murdered at age sixty-one because he spoke out against the testing and the injections being forced on the people of his country.

The governments have given themselves the power to lock down private businesses, to take away freedom of assembly, and to force citizens to wear face diapers as a symbol of submission. The governments pay the police force to enforce any random bylaw they enact; one fine day they will announce that all elections are suspended until further notice – for 'the greater good', using the guise of promoting public health. Politicians are mostly puppets who have been corrupted by the profits they make or compromised by someone blackmailing them over their recreational adventures. The people in high office do not work long hours. They have a lot of free time to indulge their hobbies and lurid habits.

The politicians invest in stocks that are a sure thing when they have inside information that certain products are going to be required by law, such as masks, tester kits, and they buy shares in companies like Zoom, Pfizer, AstraZeneca, Johnson & Johnson, and the like, whether directly or indirectly. A large percentage of people in politics, business, and medicine are atheists, so they have no reason to follow any ethics other than those they invent for themselves.

Members of the wealthy elite think they can outsmart God or push Him out of the way by calling on dark forces in Satanic rituals. They are responsible for wars and oppression because they do not fear the Creator, so all morals and conscience are forsaken in their greed for power. All things come back to a person in the end, but they fail to understand that by harming other people they are harming themselves in the long run. Every action has an equal and opposite reaction.

Victims of injustice will be compensated in the Afterlife and the guilty shall be punished many times over. They will experience the pain of their victims when their souls are locked in Hell. They will go through the anguish and pain they have caused again and again forever. The only way to avoid punishment is to ask God to forgive you and quit sinning. If you thank God for your existence and ask Him to forgive your past sins in prayer, then you have a chance at Paradise. Changing from bad to good may never happen, but at least all souls get a chance to attain Heaven.

Only the people who are capable of love will gain the reward that is waiting. It will only cost you your sins to come to God; it will cost you your soul if you fail to win God's grace. The days ahead look menacing so we must rely on our trust in the Lord to endure the tribulations that face us. The faithful will be saved and proceed to a bright future of endless knowledge and the eternal joy of Heaven.

God has said to me: "All those who are not with us are against us."

About the Author:

People have called me by the names 'Buddha' and 'Jesus', but God's name for me is "Yeshua" and He has ordered me to announce my return under the title Messiah Jesus Christ in recognition of the main teacher of spirituality, and because I did not get to live a full life span in that incarnation. I do not know people's thoughts or read minds. I cannot hear or answer prayers. God comes and goes through me like a visitor to a hut. I am the Chosen One, the first of God's creations. Mankind is to address me as "Messiah". God has given me the Keys to Heaven and Hell as First Judge of all human souls. I have no power other than what God gives me. It is God's command that I become the King of Earth, above all worldly leaders or authorities. He has given me authority over all souls and all Scripture. I can refuse entry to Heaven to anyone I feel would make me uncomfortable in eternity. It takes the open-minded innocence of a child to enter the Kingdom of Heaven. Atheists and idol worshipers will be punished for eternity in Hell. Confrontational people who judge others, those who tell lies, those who steal, and those who hold murder in their hearts will be turned away on Judgment Day. The Gate to Heaven is narrow. Your beliefs do not make you a free thinker; what makes you a free thinker is the ability to change your beliefs based on new information.

All humans must obey me and show me respect. You will address me as "Messiah", for it is written: "Those who do not honor the son do not honor the Father who has sent him." God has given me the authority to turn away any soul with whom I would be uncomfortable for all eternity, so those who deny my existence or insult me will be sent to Hell forever.

Also by Patrick Boardman

The Nature of Energy
The Golden Blues
Religion of Buddhism for the 21st Century
Doug Ford's Criminal Government
Return of Jesus Christ
Messiah Jesus Christ Reawakened

Watch for more at messiahjesusbible.com.

www.ingramcontent.com/pod-product-compliance
Ingram Content Group UK Ltd.
Pitfield, Milton Keynes, MK11 3LW, UK
UKHW022217230426
12048UKWH00016BA/895